8 WEEKS TO A COMPLETE NOVEL

WRITE FASTER, WRITE BETTER, BE MORE
ORGANIZED

BECKY CLARK

First paperback edition April 2020

Cover design by Steven Novak

ISBN (paperback) 978-1-7346893-0-3
ISBN (ebook) 978-1-7346893-1-0

www.BeckyClarkBooks.com

Excerpt from Save the Cat by Blake Snyder provided courtesy of Michael Wiese Productions.

I am indebted to Libbie Hawker, Randy Ingermanson, Mary Carroll Moore, and Chuck Wendig for granting permission for the use of their excerpted work.

For writers everywhere. Keep telling stories.

WHY THIS BOOK? WHY NOW? WHY ME?

I WAS EATING MY LUNCH … OR WAS IT SECOND BREAKFAST? … with the gang from NPR and I caught part of a story about Hans Fallada, a bestselling German novelist arrested by the Gestapo back in the day because he wouldn't join the Nazi Party.

Personally, I can't blame him. I hear they never even serve guacamole at those parties.

Anyway, I found out two astonishing things about this inspiring man.

First, Goebbels ordered Fallada to write an anti-Semitic novel. "He pretended to write the assignment for Goebbels, while actually composing three encrypted books—including his *tour de force* novel "The Drinker"—in such dense code that they weren't deciphered until long after his death."

Knowing how hard it is to write a novel, can you imagine writing *encrypted* novels? Three of them? While imprisoned by Nazis? With no guacamole in sight?

Fallada survived the ordeal and was freed after the war. His publisher wanted to help him recover and get him back to writing so he gave Fallada the Gestapo file of a couple who worked in the Resistance. Their story inspired him and he wrote "Every Man Dies Alone" in twenty-four days.

Read that sentence again. Twenty-four days.

Fallada's son said that Hans Fallada had an iron-clad rule: "No day will you write less than yesterday."

That is a high bar to reach.

I've always written my first drafts fast. Not twenty-four days fast, but pretty fast. I've also always outlined, which speeds up the process tremendously. If you're not quite on board with outlining, and the thought of it gives you sweaty-palmed hookey-spooks, think of the outline as your first draft, or a pre-writing exercise. We'll talk more about this. Lots more.

For me, though, outlining is the only way I know how to be reliably and consistently organized enough to write at least two not-completely-terrible manuscripts per year.

I don't know your specific reasons for picking up this book. You don't yet know about my flawless dance moves and practically perfect fried chicken, neither of which could be taught in eight weeks anyway. So it probably has something to do with you wanting to write your novels faster. Maybe not in twenty-four days or even eight weeks, but perhaps.

I'm also guessing you're reading this because what you're doing now isn't quite working for you and you're on the hunt for a couple of new tools for your toolbox. Whatever your reasons, whatever your time frame, I'm going to do my best to give them to you.

Here's a quick bit about my story and why this is so important to me.

I got lucky and landed a three-book deal for a cozy mystery series, one book per year for three years. Right after that, I signed with a fabulous agent who told me she wanted me to solidify my brand by publishing two books per year so I had something coming out every six months. "Sure, of course!" I said, even though up until then I had never reliably published one novel per year and didn't even have ideas for another series to pitch to her. So, I needed a plan. And fast.

For years I had been creating and honing my process here and there, but now I had to get very serious about it.

The first thing I did was grab a year-at-a-glance calendar. I marked red for the theoretical publication date of contracted book #1. Orange for when I thought I'd have to get it to my editor. Blue for outlining, pink for writing, purple for editing. Then the next project. I made up the deadlines because I didn't know what they were yet. But that gave me a visual picture of my year. And I saw I had plenty of time. That's the beauty of calendars. They're very predictable.

Of course, *having time* and *completing projects* are two very different beasts, just like *writing books* and *getting books published* don't always go hand-in-hand. (Unless you want to see me ugly-cry, don't ask me how many manuscripts are sitting, twiddling their thumbs until I get around to doing something about them.)

Before any project is completed, there must be a corresponding amount of self-discipline, BICHOK (butt in chair, hands on keyboard), and time management skills. Lucky for you, there are oodles of tips, tricks, and advice in here about that.

Whether you want to make a career out of writing or get faster at writing—or both—these ideas will help you get lots more practice, and reach that magic 10,000 hours that Malcolm Gladwell talks about in his book "Outliers." He believes for anyone to get great at anything takes 10,000 hours of deliberate practice or apprenticeship. A system will help you do that. The more words you get under your belt and the faster you learn from your edits, the faster your future writing gets.

Career writers need to be able to produce at least two novels per year—good ones—maybe even three, and that doesn't include short stories, novellas, blog posts, and all the marketing and promotion time you'll need to spend. And, not to give you heart failure, but pull up your fainting couch, fan yourself melodramatically, and read these words in a whisper

… but recently I heard that a career writer should be putting out four books every year. Ay caramba!

The process I'm going to share with you helps me keep a good churn of ideas, outlines, synopses, drafts… what I call my "pipeline."

As I write this, I'm giving this manuscript a final review before sending it off to my freelance editor. As soon as I do, I'll turn to my publishing house editor's notes and tackle revisions on "Puzzling Ink," the first book in the Crossword Puzzle mysteries. The second book, "Punning with Scissors," is with my beta readers with a due date in about three weeks. In a couple of days, I have an appointment to talk to my audiobook narrator about the Mystery Writer's mysteries. Next week a friend is coming to help me flesh out a 12-book mystery series idea, with four 3-book arcs. I'll chew on those while I reread "Metaphor for Murder," the third book in the Mystery Writer's series that's been written for ages, but put on ice until I got my rights back for the first two books.

A pipeline. A constant churn.

The pipeline leads directly to finished books. Many authors and publishers—myself included—stockpile these books and publish them close together, one per month or so in a marketing strategy called "rapid release." It helps break through the various algorithms and create some sustained buzz for a series and an author.

When you're just starting out, you're focused on that one book to sell to one agent, who must then sell it to that one editor, who must then sell to that marketing and/or editorial board, who must then sell to those distributors, and major reviewers, and anyone else they can think of to sell to—eventually—your readers.

If you're sitting around watching the grass grow until all this happens, your career will stall out.

I got an offer for another new series, but the first book wasn't set to be released for nineteen months from signing the contract. In all honesty, all three books were written and vetted by my beta readers and freelance editor before the first one was even published.

You can write that fast, too.

Gene Wolfe, the great science fiction and fantasy author said, "You never learn how to write a novel. You just learn how to write the novel that you're writing." I absolutely agree with him because every novel I've ever written has had a different process behind it, sometimes quite drastic, sometimes just a tweak here and there, but definitely different each time.

No process is set in stone. You will hear new ideas. You will evolve as a writer. You might change genres. Your situation at home or work might change. When any of this happens, you can and should adapt as necessary.

No writing or productivity advice is magic. The magic happens when you hear something that resonates with you—where you are in your journey, the problems you're having, and the alignment with your current set of skills.

You may read this—or any other helpful guide—fully intending to change your habits or implement new ideas. But it never happens.

Why? Because you're lazy/dumb/obstinate/not trying hard enough?

No, of course not!

It's only because you weren't quite ready. But that doesn't mean you can't *get* ready, or that you won't *be* ready in a few months when your circumstances or mindset changes.

Whatever your reality is, it's perfectly fine. As you progress as a writer or an outliner or get more organized, maybe you can add another 500 words to your busy life. If you have to tread water or make incremental steps until your kids are older or until your work situation changes, then that's what you do. In the meantime, you get your systems in place, make a habit of flexing your writing muscle every day so when the stars align and your situation changes—BAM—you're ready and off you go!

Your first time doing this Novel in Eight Weeks might not work perfectly for you. In fact, it might make you want to pull out your hair, or worse, pull out mine. But you need to do it the first time to assess your strengths and weaknesses. You need to crunch all your numbers to get a baseline snapshot of your productivity. It's ambitious, no doubt about that, but even if you double this process to 16 weeks (four months instead of two), you can still produce two solid books every year, with time to spare. Seriously. Yes, YOU!

But saying, "I'm going to write my next novel in eight weeks" is very different from saying, "I'm going to put a plan in place to write my next novel in eight weeks."

The difference is subtle, but very important. Do you see it?

The first is a goal. At this point, if that's your goal, you will probably fail. And when you fail, you'll say, "I'm not good enough, smart enough, diligent enough, *whatever* enough" and you'll give up, feeling bad about yourself.

The second is a plan. If your plan doesn't work, you'll say, "Hmm. That plan didn't work because ...." and here you'll fill in the blank because your plan will be made up of many components, each of which you'll be able to analyze and tweak to get closer to success.

My point isn't to wax poetic about the virtues of outlining and organization, but rather to explain how I, and others, do it. This will provide some takeaways and tools that might resonate with you so you can write solid drafts of your novels in eight weeks, and end up with a synopsis worthy of submission to editors and agents as an added bonus.

If you're nervous about your metamorphosis from pantser (writing by the seat of your pants) to outliner, you have my permission to stop here and read "Outlining Your Novel" by KM Weiland. It's an entire book on the joys of outlining, with interviews of authors who describe their outlining processes. They all survived the experience and lived to tell the tale.

Let me take a minute and address the thoughts you're probably having right about now.

You might be thinking, "Outlines stifle my creativity. They're not organic. They're boring and much too difficult." But I pinky swear, if you stick with me through this book, I will prove to you none of that is true. Knowing your story and knowing all the little details that make up your story are two entirely different things.

Maybe you can't help but think fast writing equals bad writing. You're not alone. Lots of people—readers and writers alike—have the image in their head of the tortured, poverty-stricken genius. But let's unpack that and break it down a bit.

The more you practice anything, the better you get. Writing is no exception. Every single writing session you accomplish flexes your writing muscle and strengthens it. Each completed chapter teaches you more about completing chapters. Each completed manuscript teaches you more about completing manuscripts. Your writing education is dramatically speeded up in direct proportion to how many story arcs, character arcs, tension-filled cliff-hangers, passages of dialogue, and the like you complete.

It's logic, plain and simple. If you complete two—or three or four or more—novels in the course of a year, you will automatically write better because you've had more practice than if you only write one.

If you go to the batting cages and hit a hundred balls every day, your baseball season will be better.

If you make the same Bundt cake every day for a month, you won't have to rely on the recipe each time. Plus, I bet you'll feel more confident adding a fudge swirl or a streusel topping here and there.

If you build every table IKEA sells this year, you can bet you will forevermore wield an Allen wrench LIKE A BOSS!

You get the idea. Practice makes, if not perfect, at least prolific.

Maybe you're thinking, "I can't possibly do this."

To this I affect my finest posh British accent and say, "Don't be a daft ninny!"

OF COURSE YOU CAN DO THIS. Think of all the things you've learned in your life that were difficult but now are second nature: walking, tying your shoes, riding a bike, reading, driving a car. Writing a novel in eight weeks is just another thing that seems impossible until you start practicing.

Perhaps you're thinking, "I'm simply too busy and my life is too complicated to dedicate time every day to my writing."

To that I say, "Balderdash!" Time management is all about choices, but if you're not willing to choose *yourself* over some of the other things in your life, then your books will never get written. But if you're reading this now, it seems you've already made a choice. An excellent one, by the way.

I want to make very clear to you what this book is and what it isn't so you can decide to return it right now and not be tempted to give your bossy Aunt Becky a scathing one-star review that will make me curl into a ball and rock myself in a soothing manner in the corner.

You will get absolutely zero advice from me on the craft of writing. There will be no tutorials on adverb use, or dialogue tags, or the Oxford comma. We will not stand at the chalkboard and parse sentences, no matter how delightful that sounds.

I trust if you're reading this, you already know how to string sentences together in a pleasing fashion.

You will get no marketing advice. Well, except for my favorite, because I tend to mumble it throughout the day and in my sleep: "More books sells more books." Can't argue with that, eh? (Yes, of course you can, but don't. It was rhetorical. Save your breath.)

What you will get, though, is my best advice on how to get you from your idea to a completed manuscript as quickly as possible. You'll read different ways of outlining, tips and tricks to write faster, and time management ideas to help you wrangle your calendar and your To Do list.

I am bossy by nature but I will try my darnedest to keep the dogmatic "you musts" to a minimum. I never actually mean "you must," even if it sounds that way. It's simply shorthand for, "Listen up, O Best Beloved. You might want to seriously consider this," offered with love and tenderness from your bossy Aunt Becky who only wants the very best for you.

As the saying goes, there are many paths up the mountain. And I'm here to be your Sherpa, helping you find yours.

My way never fails to get me up Manuscript Mountain. As soon as you discover your sure-fire, never-miss, eminently doable process, your way will always get you up the mountain too. Maybe not on your first attempt. Maybe not your second. Maybe you have to break in your hiking boots on the first try. Maybe on the second attempt you wear your comfy, broken-in boots and pick a better trail. And on the third try, you had the comfy boots, the better trail, and you remembered to bring the canister of oxygen. Huzzah! You planted your flag at the summit!

Please believe me when I tell you, you will find your comfy boots and oxygen tank. You *can* write faster. You *can* write better. And you *can* be more organized.

All the timelines, calendars, and templates I talk about can be downloaded from my website BeckyClarkBook.com under the "Stuff I Teach" tab. You might want to stop here and go download it all so it's handy when we start talking about it.

Whaddaya say? You ready to dive in?

2

HERE ARE THE EIGHT WEEKS DESCRIBED

SINCE YOU'RE DYING TO KNOW

OVER THE COURSE OF THIS BOOK, WE'LL BE LOOKING AT different ways to outline, how to keep track of your progress, and ideas to help you write faster and organize your time. But first, here is an overview of what those Eight Weeks To A Complete Novel actually look like, based on a 60,000-word draft, which is a good, round, doable number.

Up front I should confess that I hate revision with the white-hot intensity of ten thousand suns. In the past, I've had to pull a single plot thread from a manuscript, only to watch in horror as the entire story sweater puddled at my feet. Revision renders me so desperately unable to function that all I can do is crawl back into bed and hibernate until someone sweeps the pile of threads away. But nobody ever does that. I'm always on my own. And I don't like it.

Other writers have told me they struggle through the first draft as if on a forced march through quicksand carrying a squirmy toddler wet from a bath.

They get excited about finally writing THE END so they can gleefully toss those pages into the air—sometimes literally—and then rearrange everything.

The idea of that makes me throw up in my mouth a little bit.

I said I don't like revision, but let's define some terms. I don't like the kind of major revisions where you subtract characters or subplots, or where you get to the end and find out *no, he wasn't the bad guy after all ... it was her!* Or *this shouldn't be set in Victorian England ... it's a space opera set two hundred years in the future!*

I'm feeling faint just saying that.

The type of revision I love, however, is the layering. Where you have the bones of your story and you get to go back and add layers of description, theme, humor ... whatever it is that makes your story yours.

That's why I shoot for about 60,000 words in the first draft. I typically write lighter mysteries, which clock in at around 75,000 words at publication. Some are shorter, some are longer, but this is what I aim at for mine.

Other genres and subgenres are different. They all have their rules, and, of course, publishing houses have their rules as well. But once you get into your system, you'll have settled into a nice rhythm for your particular word count. You'll figure out the math that works for you.

I try to hit that 75k by the time I do my final polish. Because I like that layering, I prefer to err on the side of a lower word count. Adding words is so much easier than subtracting them. Seasoning a stew a bit at a time is much easier than dumping in too much paprika. There's no easy way of unpaprika-izing your stew. Don't ask me how I know this.

Here's what your eight weeks will look like.

Week 1 —outline and synopsis

Week 2 — write

Week 3 — write

Week 4 — write

Week 5 — write

Week 6 — editing

Week 7 — editing

Week 8 — final polish

I often use "outline" and "synopsis" interchangeably. That's because, to me, they're kind of the same document. Technically, though, you begin with the outline which is sparse. It gets fleshed out into the synopsis, which is a more complete version of your outline, in paragraph form. My outlines are 5-ish pages which morph into a 30-ish page synopsis. So, when I talk about a "30-page outline," don't have a cow, man.

I typically only write two or three hours a day on the days I write, but I don't put any time parameters to creating the outline and synopsis in Week 1. That's because I spend as much time as I can on the beats of my story in that first week. I find it the most fun, discovering where my story actually is and thinking about all the different directions the plot can go. I enjoy the writing and editing parts too, but I find them more difficult and demanding. Kind of like leafing through a cookbook versus settling down to prepare something for dinner. All these food references. I must be hungry.

This outlining and synopsis phase is where I'll add extra time if I have that luxury.

I'd encourage you to try this process completely my way, at least your first time through, just to give it a chance. Sometimes we need something new to shake us out of a rut or to show us we can do something we're not convinced will work. Again, you wouldn't be reading this if you had a system that was working for you. And admit it … you're curious. You want to see if you can challenge yourself this way. That's perfectly fine. Multitudes of successful projects have begun with a dare. The moon shot. Silicon Valley businesses. My haircut.

I'll probably say this forty-leven gazillion times. You *will* find your own way with this. My specific way won't work for everyone. You need to put your special spin on it, playing to your strengths and accommodating your weaknesses. But until you know what exactly those strengths and weaknesses are, you'll just be dog-paddling in the Eight Weeks pool.

We'll talk more about the outlining process later, so let's move on to the writing weeks.

You get four weeks to write your 60k words.

If you write seven days a week, you must complete 2,143 words per day to reach that goal. It's just math.

7 days in a week x 4 weeks = 28 days

60,000 words ÷ 28 days = 2,143 words/day

But say you want to take weekends off. Then ... 5 days x 4 weeks = 20 days

So ... 60,000 ÷ 20 = 3,000 words/day

Or, if you're like me and take Wednesdays AND weekends off, then 4 days x 4 weeks = 16 days

So ... 60,000 ÷ 16 = 3,750 words/day.

Before you ask, no, I don't always hit that number. But mostly I do, and sometimes go over. Sometimes I can lift entire scenes from my synopsis, pasting them directly into my manuscript. That's fun.

Remember, though, just because this week you wrote all seven days doesn't mean you have to do the same thing next week. And just because you only *wrote* four days every week doesn't mean you can't *edit* for seven days. You choose the schedule that works for you.

Or think of it the opposite way. Instead of the total word goal, what about thinking of it as a per day word goal.

If you can write 500 words/day for 6 months you'll end up with 90,000 words.

But what if you increase that to 1,000 words/day for 6 months? That's, um, close to 180,000.

Sheesh, that's a long book, so what if you just wrote 1,000 words/day for 4 months? That gets you 120,000 words. In other words, TWO first drafts.

Again, it's just math. And the sooner you find out how many words you can reliably write in an hour, the sooner you'll know how fast you can get your books written. And the sooner you know that, the sooner you can start pushing yourself just the teensiest bit more to get even faster.

Never forget that success begets success, whether it's learning to tie your shoe or writing novels. The more you write, the better you write. The better you write, the faster you write. The faster you write, the more you write. The more you write, the better you write. The better you write ... well, it never ends, does it?

However you've done it, you've now finished your four weeks and your 60,000 words. And, by the way, you've also just won National Novel Writing Month (NaNoWriMo), even though it's probably not November, so picture me doing a Snoopy dance for you while tossing confetti and handing you a balloon bouquet.

But don't celebrate for too long, because you have two weeks of editing in front of you.

The numbers I'm using for the illustration will definitely change for you, because of the actual number of pages you wrote. Again, just math.

There are roughly 250 words on a page that is double-spaced, has one-inch margins, and uses 12-point Times New Roman. Therefore, 60k words translates to about 240 pages. For record-keeping of our editing progress, we switch to PAGES per day rather than WORDS per day.

If you edit 7 days per week, then to get through 240 pages in 14 days you must complete 18 pages/day.

If you edit 5 days per week, you must edit 24 pages/day.

If you edit 4 days per week, you must edit 30 pages/day.

Obviously, you'll re-jigger these numbers based on the actual number of pages you ended up with after your four weeks of writing.

Those numbers might seem overwhelming, but because you'll be writing this draft with the help of a detailed outline, those numbers really aren't too scary. You won't be pulling threads and leaving your story sweater on the floor.

When I talk about "editing" here, it's a light edit: grammar, usage, typos, word choice. Not revision where you might remove a character or change from first person POV to third, or relocate chapter twelve. You've already done your "revision" during your outlining and synopsis phase, before you even start writing. Revising thirty pages is much easier and more efficient than revising 300 pages.

So now you've finished your two weeks of editing, and only have one week left until completion of your shiny new manuscript.

The polishing week is where you get to layer in better writing. For me, I write pretty spare description, so when I polish, I add much more of it throughout my narrative. You may have this same tendency, too, or you may want to layer in your theme or motif notes, or punch up your dialogue, or add more detail ... or all of the above.

But, Becky, you ask, what's the difference between editing and polishing?

Settle down. I'm getting to that.

When I talk about editing, you must remember that you have not seen any of your words since the day you wrote them. When we write quickly like this, there is absolutely no time for editing as you go. We'll talk later about ways to write faster, but I'll give you one little tidbit that speeds me up tremendously: using placeholder words.

As you're whacking at the keyboard getting your story down, never, never, *never* struggle to find the right word. If it's not there at your fingertips, just type in a word that's close.

In Fiction Can Be Murder, I wrote this:

Melinda Walter settled her lean Pilates body—the maintaining of which took all her free time and could fund North Korea's military for a year—into the soft leather driver's seat of her sleek red 1959 classic Corvette.

It pleased her to know she lived in an area of Denver where she could keep a car like this unlocked overnight. Her husband begged her not to, but Melinda did whatever she pleased. Besides, she'd never had any trouble. Of course, it helped that she and her husband lived behind sturdy walls with a generously compensated twenty-four-hour guard patrolling the neighborhood. God bless America.

But in my draft, it looked more like this, but with twenty percent more typos:

Melinda Walter settled her [totally in shape body] into the [comfy] driver's seat of her [red?] Corvette.

[She was happy] she lived in a part of town where she could keep her car unlocked overnight. Her husband [complained], but Melinda did [whatever she wanted]. Besides, nothing [bad] ever happened before. Of course, it helped that they lived behind [big] walls with a security guard.

All those words in brackets I knew I wanted changed in editing, but I didn't stop to gaze at my navel until the perfect word came to me. I plowed through.

Also in editing I fix my typos. If I come up with the perfect description or make the final decision on the color of her car, I add that too. If you were to read my edited version you'd smother me with faint praise. "Hm. Melinda Walter has a nice car, lives in a nice part of town. That's … nice."

You wouldn't be wowed.

That's where the polishing comes in.

"Lean Pilates body … I know this lady … North Korea, that's funny … oooh, I can feel my butt in that leather seat …."

You get the idea. You take the most basic, prosaic draft that you did in your writing phase, edit it into something more interesting, then polish it until certain words and phrases gleam. *Bing, bang, boom.*

But you only get to the *bang* and the *boom* if you power through and allow yourself to be boring and banal while you draft. You will get at least two more chances to make your words sing themselves right off the page.

By the time you've completed your two editing weeks, your 240-page manuscript will have swelled, so let's use 300 pages in our math example for the polishing week.

Again, don't look at these numbers and freak out. You're

sweeping an already clean floor, not scrubbing years of tene-ment grime.

Polishing 300 pages over 7 days = 43/pages per day

Polishing 300 pages over 5 days = 60/pages per day

Polishing 300 pages over 4 days = 75/pages per day

Let me reiterate, just because you only wrote four days per week, doesn't mean you can't edit and polish all seven days.

That's mostly what I end up doing since writing takes so much concentration, creativity, and focus. I find the editing and polishing much less taxing—physically and mentally—so I can do it every day for many more hours and just fly through the pages.

So that's the basic framework of the eight weeks.

Here's a recreation (because the original pages are a scribbly mess) of what my record-keeping looked like while I was writing my mystery PUZZLING INK.

Project: Puzzling Ink				Month/Year: June 2019 and July		
Sunday	Monday	Tuesday	Wednesday	Thursday	Friday	Saturday
I'd already written /3s for the proposal	written 50	1: 1114 4 2: 808 3: 916 ~~838~~ wph: 946 total words: 13714 16,712		1: 1054 6 2: 2994 3: 359 4407 wph: 1489 21,030		
	1: 1109 10 2: 1112 2221 wph: 1110 23,251			1: 2245 13 wph: 2245 25496		
				1: 786 20 2: 936 1722 wph: 861 27,218	1: 1054 21 2: 989 3: 953 2996 wph: 999 30,214	
	1: 1424 24 2: 1191 3: 730 3345 wph: 1115 33,559	1: 1128 25 2: 1132 2260 wph: 1130 35,819			1: 890 28 2: 901 1791 wph: 896 37,610	
		Adam's wedding festivities!!		1: 979 July 11 2: 1005 3: 872 2856 wph: 952 40466		

17

Project: Puzzling Ink   **Month/Year:** July/Aug 2019

Sunday	Monday	Tuesday	Wednesday	Thursday	Friday	Saturday
	1: 1210 July 15 2: 1248 3: 739 3197 wph = 1066 43,663	1: 1365 16 wph 1365 45,028		1: 1238 18 2: 1240 2478 wph = 1239 47,506		
	1: 1227 22 2: 1015 2242 wph 1121 49,748	1: 1718 23 2: 832 2550 wph= 1275 52,298		1: 1287 25 2: 880 2167 wph 1084 54,465	1: 995 26 2: 929 20min: 353 2277 wph = 977 56,742	THE END
first revision begins	Editing Aug 5 1: 15 pgs 2: 17 pgs 32 pages per hour 16	1: 15 6 2: 13 3: 10 4: 15 53 PPH 13-25		1: 12 8 2: 10 3: 8 30 PPH 10	1: 12 9 2: 14 3: 14 40 PPH 13	
	1: 16 12 2: 7 23 PPH 11.5	1: 15 13 2: 11 3: 13 39 PPH 13				
Second Pass thru, dealing w/ sticky notes	1: 11 19 2: 15 3: 21 4: 23 70 PPH 17.5	1: 32 20 2: 11 3: 24 4: 14 5: 24 6: 27 142 PPH 24	typing changes 21 1: 22 2: 18 3: 27 4: 16 5: 21 104 PPH 21	typing 22 1: 9 2: 27 3: 4 4: 25 65 PPH 16	typing 23 1: 11 2: 25 3: 13 49 PPH = 16 total words 65,296	

Project: Puzzling Ink   **Month/Year:** Sept 2019

Sunday	Monday	Tuesday	Wednesday	Thursday	Friday	Saturday
		Sept 3		5	6	
		total of 10 hours incorporating beta readers' comments/notes into appropriate places in manuscript (in margins, sticky notes, etc.)				
typing, writing, responding to notes	1: 7 pgs 9 2: 19 3: 27 4: 48 5: 25 126 PPH 25	1: 10 10 2: 22 3: 1 4: 14 47 PPH 12		1: 25 12 2: 27 3: 5 4: 5 62 PPH 15.5	Reading 13 6 hrs 206 pgs 34 PPH	Reading 14 2 hrs 60 pgs 30 PPH
	2 hrs tweaking 23 & fixing formatting SENT TO NORMA	74,374 words				
		Oct 1 Due to Norma				

You'll see I had about 14k words to begin with because I'd already written them as part of the series proposal package to my editor. From there, it was 17 days of writing (37 hours) between June 4-July 26 with an average WPH (words per hour) of 1148. (You'll also note my son got married during that time.)

The editing and polishing ran for 20 days (62 hours) between August 5-September 12 with an average pages per hour of 12. This manuscript was a bit different because my beta readers worked some magic and got their comments to me extraordinarily fast and I was able to incorporate them during this time. Then a couple of days for my read-through, some time to let it rest, and then a few more hours of tweaking before I sent it off to my editor a week early.

The more you follow and quantify a system (this one or any other), the better you'll know exactly where your sweet spot is.

But you won't know your sweet spot without some experimentation. You'll want to figure out how and where and when you work the best.

Do you work better when you focus for an hour, or when you use three 20-minute writing sprints with a 2-minute break between each?

Did your 2-minute breaks stretch into 5 or 10, or were you disciplined enough to just drink a glass of water, or hula hoop for one song, or give the dog a cookie and do a couple of stretches?

Writing sprints are exactly what they sound like. Set your timer and write without breathing the entire time. Okay, maybe go ahead and take time to breathe, but nothing else. Not even a sip of water. Just writing.

Sprinting might be for you if you can't shut up your inner editor or ignore distractions. Sometimes it's also what your family and friends need. "I'm getting ready to sprint. Talk to you in twenty."

Sprinting can be a great training ground to get you—and them—to hour-long uninterrupted writing sessions.

Some practiced sprinters get 1,000 words in a twenty-minute sprint. Some sprinters find sprinting with a group of good sprinters energizing and motivational. Some people (waves hand wildly in air) find it a tad demoralizing to be the slowest in the group.

But you'll never know until you try! You might have an epiphany and sing praises to the writing gods when you smoke those other sprinters.

Only you can know if it will give you friendly competition or paralyzing defeat. Facebook has some sprint groups or you might try sprinting with friends BUT STAY OFF FACEBOOK.

If you want to find some sprinters to sprint with, post a comment in the "8 Weeks to a Complete Novel" Facebook group.

This is the kind of stuff I set it up for ... finding like-minded folks who can help you, and who you, in turn, can help. One thing about the writer's journey ... no matter where you are, there are always people ahead of you and behind you. Reach one hand forward and one hand back and magic can happen for you.

Try both sprinting and focusing for an hour for a couple of writing sessions and see which feels more natural and which delivers more words. Don't think it has to be one way or another, though. You can mix-and-match your process. If you have an hour to write, write for an hour. If you have twenty minutes, sprint.

Your process never has to be *either-or*. It can always be *both-and*. Remember that.

If you don't know when your most productive times are, experiment. You may just *think* you're more productive when you write late at night. Have you tried recently to write in the wee hours before work or before the kids get up? You may simply be in the habit of writing at a certain time, but if you've been writing for any length of time, you're a different writer now. If you're new to this writing thing, you won't know when you're most productive. So find out!

Take a few weeks and try different writing schedules. Late

at night? Early in the morning? Twenty-minute sprints throughout the day? You may be surprised.

I'm an early bird, up every day at 5 a.m. But when I tried to write then, it was a fiasco. That was not efficient writing time for me, which surprised me.

And what about where you write? Take a stab at writing in a different place for a while—coffee shop, kitchen table, lounging on the couch, library, your desk, grocery store produce department. Again, keep an open mind and you may be surprised at your results. But you'll never know until you try. Be sure to keep meticulous notes of your experiment, you scientist, you.

When you're able to set aside those times and places when you're consistently more productive and the writing comes easier, your process will be a dream. This is why we do such specific record-keeping, so you know exactly what happened every single time you worked on your book. We will talk more about record-keeping as well, because it's important.

All of these numbers are goals, by the way. Some days you'll meet them, some days you'll surpass them, some days you won't. And sometimes they just won't add up to what you want. If you've followed your entire outline, got to the end of your story and you've only got 45k words, don't worry. That just means you get to layer in more description, more action, more theme, maybe add a subplot.

Remember, unless you're a literary masochist, it's much easier and more efficient to add to a story than to pull threads and unravel it.

What if you get to the end of your eight weeks and you're still not done with your draft? That absolutely might happen the first time you do this. Your job is to figure out why. You should be checking in with yourself every single hour, every single day. Did I get the words I promised myself today? Why not? Can I write an extra day this week or an extra 500 words today? 1,000? Am I making the mistake of editing as I go? What's getting in the way of my progress?

Perhaps your outline wasn't complete enough. The times I get slowed down are when I get cocky and don't fully flesh out a scene in my outline. In "Foul Play on Words," I glossed over kind of a pivotal plot point near the climax. I hadn't thought through my protagonist's motivation so I got stuck. I knew what was going to happen, but I forgot to draw that line for myself from Point A to Point B, so I floundered. I had to go back to my outline and synopsis, think it through, then get back on track. You do that enough and you will surely learn a lesson.

As with all new ventures, you might need a settling in period. If you've never attempted anything like this before, then your first time will be simply to quantify, get your baseline numbers, and ascertain your strengths and weaknesses.

It's not a failure—it's learning. Don't freak out or beat yourself up, and for heaven's sake, don't give up. It's just the first step.

If you're not meeting your goals, you need to reassess and redo your plan as necessary. Your goals should be challenging but achievable. As you get to be a better and faster writer, you'll tweak your goals, always pushing yourself. You'll begin to figure out what's challenging for you and what's easily achievable.

You may find your sweet spot where you can write 2,000 words per hour ... or 5,000. I've heard of magical creatures who can consistently achieve numbers like that—and more. If I ever meet one, I will ask for their magic elixir and pay them many pieces of gold doubloons in return. (Do gold doubloons come in pieces? I have no idea.)

If you're one of those magical creatures who can rack up tons of words every hour, you can spend more time on your outline or research or editing, or perhaps get your novel done in six weeks instead of eight. But you won't know until you track for a while, and experiment.

Even though I'm a "full-time writer"—a misnomer if ever I heard one—I only write three-ish hours per day and I take off Wednesdays and weekends. I can get several books written in a year over the course of twelve hours or so of concentrated effort every week.

You may have a demanding full-time job or a demanding family, or both, but I bet you can squeak out some hours every week for yourself. Lunchtime? Early mornings before work or before the kids get up? After they go to bed? When they nap? One full Saturday or Sunday? Can you find an hour each day to call your own? Or three half-hours? Or several 15-minute writing sprints?

If you're pumping your fist in the air yelling, "Yes I can!" then yay you. But if you're on the verge of melting into a quivering ball of angsty writer goo, please get hold of yourself because in the second half of the book, I think you'll find some ideas, tips, and tricks that will help you write faster and organize yourself for success.

Because if I can do this, you can too. There's absolutely nothing special about me, unless you count my almost perfect fried chicken or my sweet, sweet dance moves. I'm not one of those magical unicorns who can pound out ridiculously high word counts every day. I don't care to be at my computer for long stretches. I watch TV and movies every day, I meet friends for lunch, I volunteer, exercise, and garden—in short, I have a real life. But I want to write books as part of my life, so I've created a system that, with a modicum of self-discipline, allows me to do it all.

You. Can. Too.

When you focus, you don't need massive amounts of time. Quality over quantity.

Here, however, is where I caution you about the "100% mindset."

Just because you miss a day or a week, you haven't failed at any of this. Life gets in the way. Well-intentioned plans go astray. Unless you have an editor breathing down your neck, allow yourself permission to take a time-out if you need one. Call an audible. Huddle up and give yourself an encouraging, inspirational half-time speech à la Knute Rockne. (Sorry. I watch a lot of football.)

You obviously want writing to be a part of your life, but you can always take a short break from it. If you're not having fun, something is wrong and you must fix it before moving forward.

Allow yourself that luxury. Find the fun again.

A MILLION* WAYS TO OUTLINE

(*not a million)

SOME PEOPLE FEEL THEIR SPHINCTER TIGHTEN UP WHEN I SAY "outline," but that shouldn't be the case. There are as many ways to outline as there are ways to write a book or prepare a chicken dinner. If you get 100 outliners in a room, there will be 105 different ways of plotting a novel.

Again, don't freak out. Outlining is simply a tool to allow you to test concepts. Does this story hold together? If it does, then your outline is also a tool to help you organize your thoughts. And if your outline shows you that your story doesn't hold together, can you fix it before spending too much time on it? Maybe your novel is really a short story. Or a trilogy.

You might already have a favorite way to outline, but we're going to look at some more. Feel free to experiment and mix-and-match. That's how I came up with my outlining template. That said, every time I outline a novel, I change it just a bit because I've heard new and different approaches that resonate with me since the last time I completed an outline. After all, with every new manuscript, I'm a different person and a different writer. My process moves forward with me, and yours should too.

That might be one of the reasons people *think* they don't like outlines. It doesn't feel organic to them. But outlines *are* organic and should allow for organic movement, those skippy side trips into plot twists, or to take a closer peek at that shiny idea, or meet that new character who popped up out of nowhere. We've all taken that path, like Red Riding Hood in the woods. She picks the flowers. She meets the wolf. But she always remembers her destination ... Granny's house.

Your outline will get you to Granny's house and not find you scratching your head, wondering how you got to a strip mall parking lot in Wichita instead.

If you've written and/or read a lot in your genre—romance, mystery, horror, YA, fantasy, picture book erotica, whatever—you've probably internalized the rules of your genre and don't even realize you've already outlined those parts of your story in your head. Those genre conventions are indelibly ingrained and you think about them all the time, even when you're not thinking about them. So when it comes time to write, you've got your outline partially done, often without writing down a word.

You also do this when you're *not* writing in your genre, but when you get some premise or character that grabs you by your lapels and refuses to let go until you tell their story.

When I first began trying to figure out this writing thing, I asked a bunch of my prolific writer pals—maybe fifty people in various genres—if they outlined or not.

75% of them immediately said yes .... 25% said no.

But when I asked the "non-outliners" follow up questions, or asked them to describe their process, they're ALL outlining, whether they call it that or not.

They told me:

• "I interview my character and she tells me how she'd react to the premise."

- "I know how my couple will meet, what will keep them apart, and how they'll ultimately get together in the end."
- "I know the crime, the victim, the killer, the clues, and the red herrings."

Folks, those are outlines!

Just because it's in your head and not written on paper doesn't make it any less of an outline.

Some pantsers—those who write by the seat of their pants—truly believe that outlining removes the storytelling magic for them.

Elmore Leonard seems to fall into this camp. "At the time I begin writing a novel, the last thing I want to do is follow a plot outline. To know too much at the start takes the pleasure out of discovering what the book is about."

Ellen Byron, award-winning mystery author, disagrees with Leonard, telling me, "He's assuming one derives no pleasure from plotting out a story in advance. But I, like him, get enormous pleasure from discovering what my book is about. I'm just discovering it at a different point in the process than he is."

I absolutely agree with Ellen. I find it very satisfying to be able to tell my story in abbreviated form, and later, I find joy in fleshing out that story into the manuscript, making it all come alive, finishing what I set out to do originally. Plus, I find pleasure—great heaping gobs of joy, in fact—in not having to do major revisions. (Have I mentioned I don't really like revision?)

In a book called "Writing Mysteries," Tony Hillerman, award-winning author of many excellent detective novels, said he didn't outline because he couldn't think about all the details needed in a novel. But before he started writing he said he has, "a setting with which I am intimately familiar .... A general idea of the nature of the mystery .... A theme .... One or two important characters in addition to the policeman/protagonist."

I contend this is an outline. You don't need to—and can't

possibly—know all the details up front. That bit of magic happens when you're writing.

If you're feeling claustrophobic about outlines, take a deep breath. Fill your lungs with the cleansing aroma of novel structure, that solid foundation upon which your book is built.

If you're building a house, and you get the basement dug and the walls framed, think how much easier drywalling and roofing will be than if you started with the roof, then dug the basement, then called someone about maybe putting a pool in the yard.

I've tried pantsing a story without any kind of roadmap. But for me, revision is so awful and wastes so much time, I knew I had to develop a more efficient model for the few hours I have available to spend on writing.

I come by this aversion honestly, in case you were wondering. When my mother calls me, she has a note near her phone. I can hear her ticking off the items of conversation for that day. Years after my father retired, he continued to carry a briefcase, which mostly held his to-do list and a yellow legal tablet of items to bequeath us when he died. Mind you, he started this list forty years before he died. There were some fairly substantial edits over the years. Especially when one of us annoyed him.

We are a list-making, map-following, read-the-manual kinda family.

But let me say it again ... if you're a pantser and that is getting the job done for you, I applaud you. There are a zillion ways to write books and if you found one that makes sense to you and you can depend on every time, then YAY! But I suspect if it were *really* getting the job done for you, you wouldn't be reading this book.

Throw away any preconceived definitions and ideas of what an outline SHOULD look like. You don't have to have a highly symmetrical page with Roman numerals marching in soldier-straight columns like you were taught in 7th grade, unless you want them. It's a perfectly acceptable and time-honored way to organize your thoughts. And, remember, an outline—any outline—is just a way to organize your thoughts. If it was good enough for Tiberius Gracchus, it should be good enough for us, amirite?

Let's talk about some other popular ways to outline. Remember, if you're afraid of the O-word, just call it "pre-writing."

I've only curated books I've read or am familiar with, which you'll find in the Resources section at the end, but I'm sure there are a zillion others to help you find your perfect outlining system. But I beg of you, don't fall down the dark and bottomless rabbit hole of reading every single craft book published before you dive in to this. That's just another way of procrastinating and will not serve you well.

We'll talk about these types of outlines and many more:
- The Hero's Journey
- Step Outlines
- Character Arcs
- The Snowflake Method
- "W" Plotting

• and the one I use and will begin with because I love it so, my version of Blake Snyder's Beat Sheet.

4

OUTLINE EXAMPLE I

BLAKE SNYDER'S BEAT SHEET

A LITTLE BACKSTORY HERE. I DO A LOT OF THINGS RIGHT—SOLID dialogue; humorous, interesting scenes; flawed and relatable characters you want to hang out with. Unfortunately, back in the day, maybe 2010 or so, I hadn't really learned how to tie it all up with a plot that satisfied me.

Then I took a screenwriting class over the course of a couple months that a friend was required to teach as part of her MFA practicum. I went to help her fill a seat with a warm body but also because I was curious about the screenwriting process. I had been hearing for years about the "3-Act Structure," but could never get any solid information to wrap my brain around. I had no intention of writing a screenplay, but I thought some of the techniques would be helpful in structuring my novels.

She wrung her information sponge right into my brain, where I happily soaked it up. Then one day, the heavens parted, the cherubim sang, and rays of enlightenment swaddled me in their loving embrace.

She mentioned Blake Snyder's screenwriting book "Save the Cat," where he explains his Beat Sheet. It's basically a template that breaks down an entire movie into the fifteen important beats: Opening Image, Theme Stated, Set-up, Catalyst, Debate, Break into Act Two, B Story, Fun and Games, Midpoint, Bad Guys Close In, All is Lost, Dark Night of the Soul, Break into Act Three, Finale, and Final Image. Each beat builds on the previous one and anticipates the next, all while creating roller coaster conflict and tension until you get to the final word.

Screenplays are very specific types of writing. In the early days of movies, each reel held fifteen minutes of film. Therefore, a two-hour movie had eight twists or cliffhangers which kept the audiences glued to their seats while the projectionist changed reels.

People who watch movies (ie, everyone) expect those eight memorable scenes in books too, so make sure you have them.

In a screenplay, each page equals roughly one minute of a movie. When I first learned about these beats, I was watching some romantic comedy with my husband. Because I was newly aware of these beats, I saw each one of them clearly. And because we have a wall clock near our TV, I could time them. I'd pause the film, and tell him what was going to happen next. Not specifics or spoilers, but just in broad strokes. "That guy's friends are going to show up in the next three minutes." … "Here is where everything falls apart for her." My husband thought I was some sort of enchantress. To this day, he gazes upon me with awe. Pretty sure that's why, but it might be the fried chicken.

Back when I took this screenwriting class, I wrote books for kids, so I wanted to unfold my stories more cinematically. It made perfect sense to me because when I did workshops for reluctant readers, I explained that as they read a novel, they should be seeing a movie in their head. So I wanted to make sure I was writing in a way they could easily do that. When I transitioned to adults, it still made sense. Most people spend much more time watching television and movies than they do reading books, even those of us who love books. It's an ability deeply imprinted in us. Kids watch movies long before they learn to read.

It's not hyperbole to say that reading "Save the Cat" changed my life, my writing life as well as my personal life. As I became a better writer I garnered more attention which allowed me more opportunities, like being asked to teach and emcee at writer's conferences, doing book signings and speaking on panels at reader conventions. Pretty soon, most of my friends and activities revolved around the world of writing. Yes, absolutely changed my life, and definitely for the better.

With every page of "Save the Cat" I turned, everything began falling into place for me. That cartoon light bulb illuminated over my head. I had an epiphany on a mountaintop. My Patronus guided me out of the desert.

All without leaving my comfy living room chair.

Since that day, I've adapted those beats, twisting and bending them from screenwriting to novel, from Blake to Becky. They continue to serve me well. Out of all the outlining advice I've ever come across—and there's a lot—it still makes the most sense to me.

I would encourage you to read "Save the Cat," (and the new version "Save the Cat Writes a Novel" by Jessica Brody), then watch some popular Hollywood flick—not an indie because they don't always follow the rules—and follow along with a timer and a list of the beats. It will absolutely solidify the concepts in your brain.

If memory serves, my husband and I were watching "Notting Hill" or something very similar. Investigate the entire Hugh Grant *oeuvre* and I bet you'll find something to fit the bill. I recently watched the movie "Dumplin'" which is another excellent illustration of these beats.

So, when I say something about the "beats" of your story, I'm using language I learned from "Save the Cat." I hope what you'll do by reading this "Eight Weeks" book is get an overview of outlining and writing faster. Then go back and read the books I'm referencing about different ways to go about it. Come back to my book and weave your favorite way to outline into the rest of the eight week process.

When I decided to try my hand at mysteries, which can be complicated, I adapted Blake Snyder's beats into a template for myself. I incorporated extra things into it as well, from my favorite how-to books and things I'd learned from other people along the way. I needed a standard way to make sure I included all of these things in my outline, because I'm a tad forgetful.

If you're forgetful too, I encourage you to create an outline template for yourself and add whatever you need to in whatever final form your template takes. But do NOT reinvent this wheel every time. Build on your template and revise it, but don't start over with each new manuscript.

For instance, I have trouble remembering to make things worse for my protagonists. Deep down I know I need to throw rocks at them, but I was always forgetting, or maybe just subconsciously refusing because I love them so much. So in my outline, I have a reminder to tighten those screws.

I also want to make sure I have some good twists in the story so I have a reminder for that. Same with clues and red herrings. Of course in a mystery I hope I wouldn't forget clues or twists, but this forces me to think about them and decide where to place them as I'm going along.

I literally have a document I've named "Novel Template" that lives on my computer. It has all those beats and other reminders to myself. When it's time to start a new novel, I make a duplicate of my template, rename it, and off I go. I start filling in the generic beats with the specifics of my story.

While the beats have a specific order in your novel, you can move through them in any order when working on your outline. If you know the midpoint twist, start there. If you've pictured the opening scene that gets your story moving, start there. If the story you want to tell is based on the theme "there's no place like home," start there. If you have a crackerjack ending that's been blasting your brain, start there.

I usually start with just a couple of sentences for each beat, but by the time I'm at the midpoint, I've gone back to the beginning beats a few times because of something I've thought of later. "Oh, if this happens here, I need to talk about such-and-such earlier." Or I think of something better than my initial idea. (You may not be surprised to learn this happens, oh, just about all the time.) Some things, like the theme, might not be filled in until you've made several passes through the other beats, fleshing out your story.

Your salvation may not be "Save the Cat." But I sincerely believe you will find your light bulb, your epiphany, your Patronus.

Pro tip: even if you don't use Blake Snyder's beats for an outline, it's a fantastic structure for writing a synopsis. Just plug a couple of sentences into each beat, link with appropriate transitions, and you've got yourself a synopsis you can use when querying agents or editors.

5

OUTLINE EXAMPLE II

MOVIE REELS

YOU COULD ALSO DEVISE YOUR OUTLINE USING THOSE EIGHT memorable scenes from that movie playing in your head. Remember those early film reels? Perhaps they could form the backbone of your outline.

This would be a very plot-driven story, but if you have a story in mind, jot down, in order, eight big scenes—twists, calamities, cliffhangers. Then work backwards to find the characters who would best serve this story. Link each big scene with a couple of smaller scenes leading from one to the next. Voilá … outline.

6

OUTLINE EXAMPLE III

3-ACT STRUCTURE WITH A PLOTTING BOARD

I'VE BEEN HEARING ABOUT THE 3-ACT STRUCTURE SINCE I WAS A mere slip of a child of forty-one, maybe since high school, but I clearly tuned *that* out. I understood it in my head, but not in my heart. Yeah, yeah, yeah ... three acts to a story. I get it. But I didn't *get* it.

Let me remind you about the three acts.

Act One includes the hook, the inciting incident, and the slingshot of the protagonist into the story.

Act Two includes the protagonist dipping a toe in the water to begin work on their goal, the midpoint, and the protagonist thinking they're ready to confront the antagonist and meet their goal.

Act Three shows how they weren't quite as ready as they thought, the climax, and the resolution.

Sure, of course. That's a story. Whatev.

That screenwriting class I took led me to a whole new world of resources I'd never thought to explore before. There was much discussion about storyboards, because they're used in screenwriting. You've all seen one. It's basically every important thing that happens in a movie illustrated like a comic book.

It never occurred to me to incorporate something like that

into a novel outline, mainly because I can't even draw recognizable stick figures. But then Blake Snyder talked about plotting boards and I could envision one that didn't involve any artistic skills at all, just some straight lines on one of those trifold cardboard doohickys that kids use for their science fair projects.

It makes sense to me because I'm a fill-in-the-box kinda gal. The middle part of the tri-fold is twice as wide as the two ends. If you draw a line straight down the middle of this center section, you'll have four columns. A line across the equator gives you eight squares.

You can label them any way that makes sense to you.

I like, across the top:

- *Set Up*
- *The Game is Afoot*
- *Stakes are Raised*
- *Reframe Their Thinking/Plan*

And across the bottom:

- *Inciting Incident*
- *Midpoint complication*
- *False Defeat or False Victory*
- *Climax*

Okay. So what. Big deal.

Here's the Big Deal, for me, anyhoo.

Blake Snyder says you need all the beats within forty scenes. You can have more, of course. But here, in front of my face, is a tactile piece of cardboard divided into four columns, which pretty clearly, even to the mathfully-challenged, means ten scenes in each.

I could place all of my beats into each of those boxes!

It made me dizzy with joy and comprehension.

I already said that screenplays have more precise rules

about length than novels do. Novels can run anywhere from Hemingway short to George R. R. Martin long. But each page of a screenplay equals one minute of movie. Screenplays are almost always 110 pages. Blake Snyder, after years of studying movies and screenplays, assigned each of his beats to the appropriate page number, and someone, bless their nerdy little heart, created BeatSheetCalculator.com where you can go in with your 90- or 145- or 782-page screenplay and see exactly where the beats should occur.

When I finished my first novel draft using Blake Snyder's beats, guess what I did? Yep. I plugged my final page count into the Beat Sheet Calculator. Then I saw if my beats came close to where they should be. I didn't agonize over the *exact* page, but I wanted to make sure it was in the vicinity. If it wasn't, I tried to figure out why. Sometimes I didn't care, because I had necessary dialogue or description. But a couple of times I decided to move a scene forward or backward.

Remember how much I hate to do that? Pull that thread and unravel my sweater right there on the floor?

So I tweaked my outline template to include page numbers for each beat. The sweet spot for my mysteries is 75,000 words, which at 250 words per page, works out to a 300-page manuscript. So I plugged 300 pages into the Beat Sheet Calculator and voilá again ... a better roadmap. Now as I'm writing, I can eyeball my beats and my page count at the same time to keep on track from the get-go.

Back to the science fair cardboard.

Now you get to unwrap a gorgeous package of pristine index cards, white or multi-colored, your choice. Fondle them, explore their smoothness and pokey corners, debate the merits of their lined sides versus their blank sides. Now the hard part. Count out forty of them. Thank the rest for volunteering and assure them there will be ample opportunity for their service in the future. You have many novels to write, after all. Introduce your chosen forty cards to your favorite pencil.

Use one card for each scene you think you need. Brevity counts here, folks. Just the scene high point. If you know your story fairly well, your brain will fill in the location, the emotion, and the conflict every time you read that card. But if you want to add the details, and can do it briefly, then by all means do it.

Your card might say:

Backyard retirement party – daytime
Cassidy thinks she sees her long-lost niece.
Starts out surprised, ends up determined.
Cassidy wants to find out; sister doesn't

In the same way you don't have to work through Blake Snyder's beats in the order they're laid out, you don't have to write the index cards in chronological order, either.

You might have a great 'introduce the hero' scene or finale or midpoint twist, which is why you wanted to write story in first place. Get these on your index cards and pin them to the board where you think they go. Then use the rest of your forty cards to flesh out the story in the appropriate spaces.

For outlining purposes, I'd suggest hitting the inciting incident, the midpoint, and finale early on. You probably know what those entail, at least in broad strokes, and you know exactly where they go. As you're adding scenes, it will become perfectly clear what has to come before and after the midpoint.

You can even color-code—by ink or index card color—to track certain characters or locations or subplots. Whatever makes sense to you. Just understand the plotting board can be a huge time-suck if you let it. You can arrange and rearrange cards, work on your color-coding skills, and second guess yourself forever. But don't. Get a structure that makes sense and start writing because this plotting board is not set in stone. You can change things as you need to. There's always stuff you hadn't thought of until your muse strikes you when you're sitting at the keyboard. (You didn't realize muses were so violent, did you?)

As Blake Snyder says, "If your board is too perfect, or if you spend too much time trying to make it so, then you have left the world of preparation and entered the Procrastination Zone."

The plotting board, beats, and scene cards let you play with the elements of your novel without committing to any of them. You're simply preparing, experimenting, and testing.

You don't need to use the science fair cardboard. You can put this same information on a whiteboard, or corkboard, or paint the grid on a wall in your office, or buy huge rolls of butcher paper to attach to your ceiling so each piece drops down and you have to walk through the forest of your story hacking your way through scenes as you make your way to your desk ... again, whatever makes sense to you.

Or use Post-it notes instead of index cards.

Or write your index cards, but put them on a table or the floor. Look down upon your forty cards from the heavens as the God of Your Story might.

Of course, you can also outline using the 3-Act Story Structure without a plotting board or index cards.

OUTLINE EXAMPLE IV

3-ACT STRUCTURE IN PROSE FORM

HERE, YOU'RE USING THE SAME STRUCTURE, BUT NO INDEX CARDS or plotting board. Just words.

In prose form, write your Act One—a few sentences describing the hook, the inciting incident, and the first plot point to send your protagonist into the story.

Next, your Act Two. Write about how your hero tentatively begins to work through this problem to reach their goal. What's the midpoint? Will they have a false victory or a false defeat? How will they double down, now more confident about their goal and/or their antagonist?

Finally, write your Act Three. How do they hit rock bottom? How do they rise above it? How do they win? Write your climactic scene and the ending.

That's an outline. And a synopsis, if we're being technical.

OUTLINE EXAMPLE V

MIND MAPPING

I'M PRETTY VISUAL, SO I OFTEN USE A MIND-MAPPING TECHNIQUE —essentially brainstorming + doodling—to flesh out my characters' relationships with one another, how their secrets and lies intertwine, maybe how their motivations crash into one another. It's particularly helpful when you have a large cast of players.

I found a kid's oversized drawing pad in the office supply aisle of my grocery store. I plop myself down on the floor with it and my colored markers in front of me. Well, I used to plop down on the floor. Now I stand at my breakfast nook so I don't have to hear my chiropractor admonish me about things a woman of a certain age simply shouldn't do.

The protagonist's name goes in the center with all the main characters branching off, with other secondary characters branching off from them. I jot down whatever I'm mapping—secrets? lies? motivations? relationships?

By the time I'm done, I have a one-page graphic representation of a huge chunk of my story.

You can also use this mind-mapping technique as a plotting tool as well.

Write your inciting incident in the center of the page and

draw a box around it. For my amateur sleuth mysteries, that would probably be the first murder.

Then, like spokes on a poorly-designed, oddly-shaped wheel, add other boxes.

Off the MURDER box would be a line labeled VICTIM. Branching off from the victim I'd want to know their secret, their relationship with the sleuth, and their relationship with all the innocent suspects. I'd draw a box with each innocent suspect with lines to each one's lies, secrets, alibis, motives, opportunity. And there'd be intersecting lines. How do the innocent suspects know the victim, the sleuth, and the killer? From the SLEUTH box I'd have spokes explaining why they'd investigate this murder, who wants them to, who doesn't want them to. I'd have a box or two for allies and main secondary characters with lines and boxes about how they're going to help the sleuth, and how they'll thwart them. I'll have boxes for clues: how will the sleuth find them, are they reliable, are they red herrings? And a ton of information about the killer and the crime.

You get the idea. When you're done, it will be a glorious mess.

Of course, it doesn't all need to be on one page. You could mind map the characters and all their relationships on one page. On another, map out all the clues. On another, focus on the murder.

Or in the center of one page write INVESTIGATION. Draw your plot points, subplots, and clues branching from each. Don't mention your characters at all.

Or use your mind map to marry your plot to your thematic elements to see if you can illustrate it all to your reader.

Visual and tactile learners particularly like this method of outlining. It is free-form and loosey-goosey frenetic. Your marker might not be able to keep up with all your ideas.

9

OUTLINE EXAMPLE VI

CHARACTER ARCS

YOU COULD ALSO DEVISE AN OUTLINE STRICTLY FROM YOUR characters. Literary types are always talking about "character-driven stories." If you know your protagonist, your antagonist, and your supporting characters inside and out, their arcs can constitute your outline. Let's think of a character arc as points on a map, as if they're traveling from Los Angeles to New York City. Nope. Scratch that. Your novel is unique. You're going from Fresno to Poughkeepsie.

So Fresno is your character's normal world. He's sad and lonely, bordering on bitter since his wife died. But he has a call to action when his daughter, Poughkeepsie, calls him in tears to tell him her landlord said she must give up her beloved Irish wolfhound, which Mom and Dad gave her as a puppy when she got her first real job. The dog isn't allowed to fly, she can't get time off from work, there are no dog-friendly rentals to be found … will he drive out to pick up the dog and bring him back to Fresno to live with him? He grumbles, but agrees.

In Indianapolis he stops for gas where a desperate child is trying to give away the litter of puppies her dog just had because her family is too poor to care for them. She begs him to please take one. He gruffly tells her he couldn't possibly do that, but hands her a twenty-dollar bill, showing us his heart might be thawing just a bit.

Between Indianapolis and Poughkeepsie, he has imagined conversations with his dead wife, showing us how he loved her and why she loved him. She reminds him when they picked out that puppy for their daughter.

In Poughkeepsie he has an awkward reunion with his daughter, and we learn why he has held her at arm's length since his wife's funeral. He picks up the dog, but not literally —Irish wolfhound, remember?—and turns around to go home.

Between Poughkeepsie and Cincinnati on the return trip, we see what kind of trouble and affection a huge dog can bring an old man, knocking him further out of his comfort zone. He speeds toward Indianapolis and that gas station.

Does the old man's story end in Indianapolis? Does it continue on toward Denver? Take a detour to Winnipeg?

What about the daughter? Is her story just beginning? Was she telling the truth about her landlord? What about the wife ... where was she headed before she died? And the Irish wolfhound? The puppy? Do they have a happily-ever-after?

If you know these character arcs, you've outlined your story.

10

OUTLINE EXAMPLE VII

LIBBIE HAWKER'S "THREE-LEGGED OUTLINE"

LIBBIE HAWKER TAKES THE CHARACTER ARC A STEP FURTHER IN her book "Take Off Your Pants: Outline Your Books For Faster, Better Writing." I'm absolutely in love with this book. She explains how she uses a "Three-Legged Outline" with character arc, theme, and pacing as the central tenets. Your plot has to service those three legs equally or it wobbles, so you need to build these before you can build your plot. She believes—and makes an excellent case for—the idea that your character's flaw shapes every aspect of your book, and that every story is a character arc.

Before she begins her plot outline, she knows who her main character, antagonist, and allies are; what the external goal is; her main character's flaw; the theme; and the ending.

Using all those as her North Star, she creates her outline: opening, inciting incident, character realizes external goal, display of flaw, drive for goal, antagonist revealed, thwart #1, revisiting the flaw, new drive for the goal, antagonist attacks, girding the loins, the battle, death, outcome.

Her first book of 60,000 words took her two years to write, back when she was a pantser. Then she figured out her process and wrote a 92,000-word novel in three weeks like this. It's one of her bestsellers.

Hawker uses well-known examples (Charlotte's Web, Lolita, Harry Potter and the Sorcerer's Stone, The Cat in the Hat), to illustrate her principles, which she adapted from John Truby's book "The Anatomy Of Story: 22 Steps To Becoming A Master Storyteller."

Here's the example she gives about Wilbur's character flaw in "Charlotte's Web."

"Since one of Wilbur's greatest fears is death, he must be confronted by its specter again and again until he finally overcomes his flaw. First, he is nearly killed because he's the runt of the litter. Later, he begins a campaign, along with his barnyard friends, to establish himself as a celebrity, so that Farmer Zuckerman won't kill him for his meat. But in the climax of the book, he learns that even as a celebrity, he cannot escape death—he must confront the loss of his dearest friend, Charlotte the spider, before he can conquer his flaw and achieve his hero status. If Wilbur's flaw hadn't involved a fear of death, there would be no point in weaving this theme of confronting death and grief into the plot."

I adore this. All of the plot—every single thing that happens—in "Charlotte's Web" is driven by Wilbur's flaw, his fear of death.

If you have multiple POV characters, you should do this for each of them. I've been struggling with a complicated mystery that has, admittedly, perhaps too many characters. Before I get back to work on it, you can be darn sure I'll be re-reading "Take Off Your Pants."

11

OUTLINE EXAMPLE VIII

4-ACT STRUCTURE

WE TALKED ABOUT THE 3-ACT STRUCTURE. DID YOU KNOW there's also a 4-Act method of plotting?

Act I is where you introduce your main characters, their goals, obstacles and stakes.

Act II includes the initial try-fail cycles and early consequences. It ends with the Midpoint change-up.

Act III deals with consequences and sees bigger try-fail cycles with more dire consequences.

Act IV is where the hero uses their lessons learned, has an All is Lost moment, and gives the final push. There's either a victory or a failure, and the denouement at the end.

You could use either the 3-Act or 4-Act Structure just as a bullet list of scenes to use as your roadmap from the beginning to the end of your story.

12

OUTLINE EXAMPLE IX

WORK BACKWARDS

WHAT IF YOU HAVE A GREAT IDEA FOR AN ENDING, BUT NOTHING else? How 'bout starting with the end and working to the beginning as a way to organize your outline? You know your hero is going to have his climactic scene where he slays the dragon. But how did he get there? Where did he learn his skills? Who helped him? Who hindered him? Where did he perform this derring-do? Answering the main questions will create your backwards framework.

13

OUTLINE EXAMPLE X

THE STORY CIRCLE

THE HERO'S JOURNEY HAS SPAWNED MANY PLOTTING DEVICES, one of which is the "Story Circle" or "Plotting Circle" created by Dan Harmon that many writers use.

Just like Blake Snyder studied movies and found commonalities in screenplays, in the 1800s an anthropologist named Edward Burnett Tylor found that in hero mythology there were commonalities also. Basically, that a hero goes on a quest, hits rock-bottom somehow but claws himself up to emerge triumphant, then returns home altered in some significant way. Hero 2.0, say.

In 1949, Joseph Campbell popularized the idea of *The Hero's Journey* in his book "The Hero With The Thousand Faces."

Personally, I cannot wrap my brain around The Hero's Journey. It has never seemed germane to the stories I write, I guess because I write a lot of reluctant heroes and they don't seem to be on a journey of any kind. They're not hobbits on a quest. Or Jedis out to save the galaxy. They're just ordinary people thrust into a modern-day mystery they have to solve.

But a story circle may speak to you. Draw a circle. Write **1** at the top and **5** at the bottom; **3** and **7** are the horizontal points. Fill in 2, 4, 6, and 8 in the remaining quadrants. Now you have a clock that only goes to 8:00. Lucky for you this isn't a clock.

This is what the numbers represent:

1. Comfortable, ordinary world
2. Hero's desire
3. They step into unfamiliar world
4. Conform to it
5. Achieve their desire
6. But it cost them dearly
7. They're back in their ordinary world
8. But they're a different person

Of course, numbers 2-6 can continue to make smaller concentric circles within the greater circle, with constantly shifting desires and achievements and costs. By the time they're back in their ordinary world, they've changed in some way, big or small ... or both.

14

OUTLINE EXAMPLE XI

THE "W" PLOT STRUCTURE

MARY CARROLL MOORE IS CREDITED WITH DEVELOPING THE "W" Plot structuring tool, also based on Joseph Campbell's Hero's Journey. She explains the "W" in much more detail in a YouTube video entitled "Your Book Starts Here - Storyboarding for Writers."

The five most important points in your story are represented by the five points on your W. She calls them: Trigger Event, 1st Turning Point, 2nd Triggering Event, 2nd Turning Point, and Resolution.

The lines making up your W she calls: Setting Up The Problem, Recovering From the Problem, Deepening the Problem, and Resolving the Problem. If you can label your W with those nine ideas, you've got yourself an outline.

It's funny, it never occurred to me that Moore's plotting tool was also inspired by The Hero's Journey, until she pointed it out to me. Like I mentioned, I could never truly embrace The Hero's Journey concept. But these lines and points on a W make perfect sense to me.

I guess that's another example of what I hope you take away from this book: something, or multiple somethings, that will resonate for you to make sense of an outlining method.

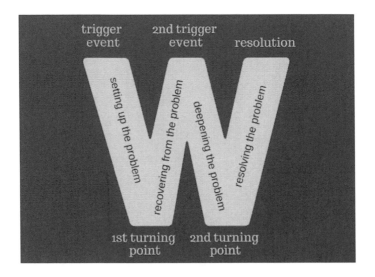

15

OUTLINE EXAMPLE XII

THE SNOWFLAKE METHOD

MANY PEOPLE FIND RANDY INGERMANSON'S "SNOWFLAKE Method" indispensable for their

outlining process. As a physicist, he based his ideas on the Koch Snowflake, a mathematical fractal.

He wants you to begin with a one-sentence hook that summarizes your story.

An orphan learns he's a wizard and is sent off to a special school to develop his powers.

A young hobbit inherits a ring that must be destroyed in the fires of Mount Doom in order to save civilization.

A teen bullied by her peers and abused by her mother finds out at the school prom she has supernatural powers.

It might seem difficult to do this without knowing your story, but I think it's a bit easier to do before you have all the details getting in your way. Like seeing a nugget of gold in your pan amid all the gravel. Seeing your forest instead of all those pesky trees.

Then you expand that sentence into a paragraph, hitting all your major plot points. Then you expand your paragraph to a page. Then to four pages and a synopsis.

Next, you paint your characters with a broad brush—

motivations, goals, conflicts, epiphanies—before creating fully-fleshed out characters.

You're building layers and arms of your story the same way ice crystals build upon themselves to create snowflakes.

Ingermanson wrote "How To Write A Novel Using The Snowflake Method" and talks about it on his website AdvancedFictionWriting.com. Take a look and see if this might create an avalanche of ideas for you. (I'm here all week, folks.)

OUTLINE EXAMPLE XIII

STEP OUTLINE

A STEP OUTLINE IS A SERIES OF, UM, STEPS THAT LEAD FROM THE beginning to the end of a story. Picture a staircase. You can choose whether it leads to a dark basement for your horror story, or a sweeping ornately curved one for your historical comedy of manners, or the polished walnut of the courthouse interior for your legal thriller, or the beige carpeted one your suburban unreliable narrator will trod.

Each step represents a major or pivotal event. Some events take several scenes, so it's not exactly a "scene outline." The important thing to remember about a step outline is that every step requires cause and effect. That causal connection is one of the fundamental concepts in storytelling. Every step forward is a consequence of the events that already happened.

Ebenezer Scrooge was a mean old miser. BECAUSE OF THAT he took advantage of his clerk and his debtors. BECAUSE OF THAT Jacob Marley, his dead business partner, wanted to spare him the fate he suffered when he went to hell. BECAUSE OF THAT Marley sent three ghosts to visit Scrooge in an effort to convince him to change his ways.

You get the idea.

OUTLINE EXAMPLE XIV

CUT AND PASTE

MAYBE YOU'RE VERY VISUAL, LIKE LESLIE KARST, THE AUTHOR OF the popular Sally Solari mystery series. Here's what she told me about the outline for one of her mysteries.

"I started with one or two big ideas or concepts, then I brainstormed conflicts, themes, and scenes that could branch out from them. I made a calendar on a legal pad and filled in the Big Scenes, then worked forward and backward from them, filling in the smaller plot points as they came to me. I typed up all my plot points, printed out the pages, and cut each idea into a strip of paper. I set them all on the dining room table and spent three days moving them around until I was happy with the order. I then taped them together in that order and had my outline. A literal cut and paste job!"

OUTLINE EXAMPLE XV

TENT POLE MOMENTS

CHUCK WENDIG TALKS ABOUT TENT POLE MOMENTS. THOSE points of your story that, if one was missing, the whole thing would crash down and suffocate you before you could even leap from your chair and rescue your coffee. He jabs each spike into the ground—"a cascading sense of consequence"— making his way around his story until he feels it's steady and won't collapse in a breeze.

As he travels around his tent, he sees the acts beginning to form. Woven through the poles and the acts, the non-tent pole moments begin to take shape, all that fun stuff that happens, what Blake Snyder calls "fun and games" in his beats. The things you see in the movie trailer.

Before you know it, you've created a solid structure to hang the rest of your paragraphs and pages on.

To get some practice seeing these tent pole moments, he suggests watching a movie, or a scene from a movie, and identifying these moments, but he also warns you not to "overbuild" or outline forever. Always a lurking danger.

He talks in more detail about the Tent Pole Structure in a blog post at TerribleMinds.com. If you can handle some salty language, you'd do well to bookmark his website because he has a plethora of writing advice for all of us "pen monkeys."

OUTLINE EXAMPLE XVI

TELL YOUR STORY OUT LOUD

IF YOU'RE MORE VERBAL, TRY TELLING YOUR STORY TO A PAL OR to a pet or to the cavernous, echoing living room. Or to the person next to you on the train. They'll love that.

I'm including this idea for two reasons.

First, not too long ago, I auditioned for a radio play that we were going to perform for a live audience. (I recognize that sentence doesn't make a whole lot of sense, but I bet you understood it anyway. Isn't English a marvelous language?)

This process involved me submitting an mp3 as my audition.

I had no idea how to do that, so I began searching until I found a free digital audio software program called "Audacity." I downloaded it, watched a short tutorial about how to use it, and after only two tries, got a perfectly respectable audition. I got the part, too! (Let's pretend I wasn't the only woman who auditioned.)

Second, after my dad died, I was tasked with organizing and curating his cassette tapes and his file cabinet of speeches. He'd been a grand poobah Toastmaster since about 1957. I never really knew his process in developing his hundreds of speeches before I started diving into his fascinating files. But now I think I've cracked the code.

His technique involved writing some notes, the thoughts that spilled out of his brain as he considered his topic. Kind of a combination of mind-mapping and Roman numeral style. Sometimes these notes found their way into a written essay of sorts. But more often than not, the notes I found were shortened and shortened until they were just the nuggets of his ideas.

At first I thought the scraps of paper covered in these nuggets were his first attempt at organizing his thoughts. But the more files I studied, the more I realized I had it backward.

In one of the cassette tapes I had digitized, I heard him rehearsing a speech I'd seen in his files. The first time through developing a speech, he wrote out everything he thought he wanted to say, something we writers call our "vomit draft." But then, before each time he rehearsed his speech into the tape recorder, he'd jot the main points.

If his vomit draft had, say, twenty points he wanted to make, the second note he jotted to himself had seventeen. The third might have fifteen, and the fourth maybe a dozen.

Every time he worked on that speech he crystalized his thinking about it until his notes were sparse, but his speech was rich.

You can do the same thing to produce an outline for your story. When you record yourself telling the story the first time, you'll have enormous plot holes, spots where you come up blank, perhaps duplication of many thoughts.

Stop recording there and open a new file. Think about it for a minute, then start recording again at the beginning. The more you tell your story, and listen to it, the better you'll be able to synthesize the major events and let go of the chaff.

Plus, you can pretend you're on a Broadway stage, enthralling an audience who paid $200 each to hear you.

Close your eyes and tell your story. If you want to channel my dad, smoke a cheap cigar while you do it.

OUTLINE EXAMPLE XVII

CHECKLIST

WHAT ABOUT JUST USING A SIMPLE CHECKLIST FOR YOUR STORY?

No matter the genre, every book needs a protagonist, a main and a couple of secondary story questions, at least one antagonist, a supporting cast, a unique setting, and enough twists to keep your reader guessing.

You've read enough books to know that every story also needs

GOALS ➜ OBSTACLES ➜ CONFLICTS ➜ RESOLUTIONS ➜ NEW OBSTACLES.

If you can jot a list of these things, you've got the basis for your story.

OUTLINE EXAMPLE XVIII

START WITH YOUR SYNOPSIS

I TOLD YOU EARLIER THAT I WRITE MY SYNOPSIS FROM MY BEATS. But what if you did the opposite? What if you outlined by writing your synopsis?

I mostly write series mysteries. But before I decide on a series, I want to make sure I have enough ideas and interest to sustain me for at least six books.

Long before drafting a novel, I create a series framework ... hook, recurring characters, setting, plot ideas, title ideas, marketing ideas.

By the time I pitch a series proposal to my agent, I know all these basics, PLUS I have an outline and 50 pages of the first novel. For subsequent novels, I just send the finished manuscript to my agent for her comments and then to my editor.

However, if I'm feeling fragile about the manuscript or I have a lot of extra time, I can run my outline and synopsis by them to get input before I write.

Just as it's easier to write and revise a 30-page synopsis, it's easier for an agent, editor, or beta reader to read and comment on it, too. It also allows them to see your vision early on so there are no surprises—and therefore no big, scary, time-consuming revisions—after it's all written.

Tell your story in a few pages. Pretend you're writing a letter to a friend about something that happened to you. Just the highlights, not a lot of detail, no tangents.

22

OUTLINE EXAMPLE XIX

EXPAND YOUR LOGLINE

ALONG THOSE SAME LINES, WHAT IF YOUR OUTLINE GREW FROM your logline? There are a bunch of different ways to organize a logline.

The first they call the Pixar Pitch:

Once upon a time, _____. Every day, _____. One day, _____. Because of that, _____. Because of that, _____. Until finally, _____.

Once upon a time, there lived a boy named Luke. Every day he helped fix droids with his uncle. One day, a droid projected a mysterious message from Princess Leia. Because of that, he meets Obi-Wan and Yoda who teach him the ways of the Jedi, his heritage. Because of that, he joins the Rebel army. Until finally, he drops the perfect shot that destroys the Death Star.

Here's another logline template:

On the verge of a (STASIS=DEATH MOMENT), a flawed hero (BREAKS INTO TWO); but when the (MIDPOINT) happens, they must learn the (THEME STATED) before the (ALL IS LOST).

After his uncle denies his request to apply to the Imperial Academy, Luke Skywalker discovers two droids with a message from the kidnapped Princess Leia. While he races to save her, he must learn the way of the Force before the Rebellion is crushed.

And another:

In a (SETTING) a (PROTAGONIST) has a (PROBLEM) (caused by an ANTAGONIST) and (faces CONFLICT) as they try to (achieve a GOAL).

A long time ago in a galaxy far, far away, Luke Skywalker is drawn into a galactic war started by Darth Vader. Luke and his rebels face almost certain destruction unless he learns to harness the power of the Force to save their planet.

Even if you don't use the logline method to outline, you might want to think about writing a logline before you start drafting your novel. Perhaps even before you finish your outline.

Think back cover copy, Amazon blurbs, Netflix descriptions. You can certainly do this at any point in your process, but it's always easier to write a blurb before all that detail starts cluttering up your brain. As your story evolves and you understand your theme or the emotion of your story better, you can always tweak your blurb. But if you have your logline or blurb posted prominently while you're writing, you can make sure you're on track with your story and haven't drifted into another lane, or worse, taken an unmarked off-ramp.

Try this right now. For the manuscript in the forefront of your brain, write a blurb and a tagline. A blurb is a few sentences, a tagline is just one. The tagline is very useful. People are busy. They may only read the tagline so you need to make sure it explains your story. You may or may not use the tagline in your blurb, but you will definitely want it for your marketing.

Blurbs should entice, not summarize. Study Netflix or any of the streaming movie services. One thing Netflix descriptions don't always do well—but you must—is match the tone and style of the story. If your book is funny, your blurb should be. If your book is a western, it better sound like a cowboy. If your book is horror and I'm not scared by your blurb, it's back to the drawing board for you.

Study the blurbs of bestsellers in your genre and subgenre. Go to Amazon and search "bestselling cozy mystery" or whatever. Then start clicking on covers. You'll see the tagline, usually in bold right under "Product Description." Then after that, you can read a few paragraphs explaining the basic plot.

Remember, though, that blurbs are not one-size-fits-all. You can crowdsource with trusted pals to tweak wording of your blurbs and taglines, but only you know the heart of your story. Believe that blurbs and loglines get easier the more you write them. Practice, if you have time, on books or movies you love. Or on books not yet written, just make stuff up and practice blurbifying.

If you can't tell your story in a few sentences, I guarantee you will have plotting problems.

So THOSE ARE SOME OF THE MORE POPULAR WAYS OF OUTLINING A novel. Did any of them spark epiphanies? Which intrigued you? Which might you want to investigate further?

Don't think you can't mix-and-match these ideas, or any others, like so many Garanimal outfits. Remember, your outlining process is as unique as you are.

However you choose to outline, I'd encourage you to start with the very basic info you have about the story you want to write, because the brain is a marvelous thing. As soon as you jot down the easy, most obvious plot points or character details, the sooner your brain starts digging deeper, working on trickier, more thought-provoking and unique aspects of your story.

According to the "South Park" guys, Trey Parker and Matt Stone, if you can insert "and then" between your beats, you've got a boring, episodic story. I think they're right when they say you should connect every scene with a "but" or a "therefore."

Have you ever heard someone (especially an eight-year-old boy) explain the plot of a movie or a dream? It's usually just a recounting of the events that took place. "There was a spaceship that came to earth? And then it started blowing things up? And then a guy tried to stop it? And then he was sucked up in the beam? And then some other guys had to ...." Gah. Make it staaahp! (When one of our sons was eight, we had to limit him to two "and thens" or else Mommy had to be limited to two shots of tequila.)

It's so much better to recount that this happens and *therefore* that happens. Or this happens *but* causes that to happen.

Your job is to find plot points that lead you toward a big therefore or to a big but. [Insert your own eight-year-old boy joke here]

Another cool thing about outlines is that they allow you to drill down to figure out where and what might be some good subplots to use.

If your research leads you to an important nonfiction element, would your readers want to know more about it? That could be a fascinating subplot.

Are there any secrets you can explore? Secrets always make good subplots.

Is your setting unique enough to warrant a subplot?

Can someone's character flaw or quirkiness lead into a subplot?

You'll be able to see all of these so much easier in a 30-page outline or synopsis than in a 300-page novel.

Before we leave the topic of outlines, I want to stress a couple of things.

First, don't wait to move forward with your outline until you have the perfect opening, for instance. Regardless of which outlining system you choose, be sure to use broad strokes to begin with. Everything will deepen as you work your way back and forth through your outline.

I think Jack Kerouac's idea of "first thought, best thought" is fundamentally wrong. To me, your first thought is just that ... an idea, a launch pad, a foundation to build on. That's why

I go back and forth over my outline and synopsis as much as I can to flesh out ideas and deepen them. Because, honestly, if you're using your first thought, it's probably your reader's first thought, too. If you're not surprising your readers, they're not going to be on the edge of their seat, eagerly turning pages to see what happens next.

That said, you have a finite amount of time to hammer out your outline so it's really important to use every available minute to get it as detailed as possible.

By the time I finish my outline, it's usually about three pages. If it's longer, great. If it's shorter, I find it will slow down my drafting phase because it typically means I haven't thought something through well enough.

When I asked my author pals how they outlined I got a ton of unique answers. Most are creating something specific to them and their skillset, combining bits and pieces from several ideas I've presented here, and some that are uniquely their own.

That's what I hope you take away from this section. Not everything will be a perfect fit for you, but *something* will strike your sensibilities. Maybe Blake Snyder's beats, maybe the Hero's Journey, maybe that snowflake. Your job is to seek further information from any of the ideas that strike your fancy. There are entire books written about most of these ideas. Let all the ideas percolate for a while, then throw them against a wall. The stuff that sticks for you will become the basis for your new outlining process.

And the beauty of that? Whatever you come up with will be perfect, because it's yours.

23

SO, NOW YOU HAVE YOUR OUTLINE

WHAT'S NEXT?

WHEN YOU'RE DONE WITH YOUR OUTLINE, YOU'RE GOING TO know all the main and secondary characters you need. Here's where you stop and name them all—first and last names— before you go any further. You can always change the names later if they're not quite right.

Put a bit of thought into your character names so they're memorable, though. Think about their qualities. I might think of a celebrity who's a diva or a jerk or dreamy and use a variation of their name ... same last name with a different first, or vice versa. Or a celebrity who's similar to the way my character looks. If I call her Meryl Something or Something Limbaugh, you get an immediate idea of how they look. But mainly, I'm naming characters for myself, often as little jokes. Like one time I needed a train employee so I called him Thomas Percival, after the Thomas the Tank Engine stories I used to read with my kids. It made me laugh and I was always able to remember his name as I was writing. Another time I had to name the owner of a fictional mountain resort. So I looked at a map of Colorado, decided where I envisioned this resort, then chose two nearby places as his first and last names.

Print a photo of each character, one per page. I use

random headshots I find on the internet, or friends and family, or celebrities. However I'm picturing these characters. It's not for anything but my own use.

Below the photo on each character template, I add specific, but brief, information about each of them. Assign each character a unique physical trait and a psychological one. They don't need to be dramatic or over-the-top, just distinctive: big feet, perfect posture, sunglasses always on their head, constantly in a hurry, vain, insecure about their hair. With just two brush strokes, you have the basis for a real person. Then add the rest.

Name:
Job:
Age:
Marital status:
Kids:
Where do they live:
How do they dress:
What do they eat:
How do they speak:
What do they do for fun:
What's their personal motto:
What are they good at:
What are they bad at:
What's their secret:
Other notes:

If they have tattoos or scars I draw them on this page. You want all their information on one side of one easy-to-refer to page. Be sure to refresh your memory whenever you start writing about them again. You don't want someone with a left leg limp to suddenly switch to his right. Or a guy with a tattoo of an anchor to suddenly sprout a butterfly tramp stamp. This is the easiest way to avoid continuity problems, which is important within each book and mandatory throughout a series.

After you have all your characters solidified, you want to do the same with your settings. Because of your outline, you know where most of your significant action will be taking place.

Draw a sketch of the town or download a map of a real place. Use that, or rename the streets. Find pictures of, or sketch, your character's apartment, office building, train station, hotel room ... any setting you mentioned in your outline.

These sketches do not need to be professional quality. Or any quality at all. They're just for you to orient your characters into their space, and as a continuity check while you write, and if it's a series, to refer to from book to book. As long as you know what it looks like, that's all you need.

Decide on the make and model of your character's car and find photos of both the interior and exterior before you start writing. Decide on the colors.

Then it's on to the next step.

24

WRITE YOUR SYNOPSIS

Now you're ready to put your outline notes into paragraph form.

Take each one of those bullet points, steps, beats, sticky notes, index cards, Roman numerals—however you did your outline—and write your story in prose form, expanding as necessary. If you have some dialogue in your head, include it in your synopsis. This is not a synopsis you'd send to an agent or editor. This one is just for you for now.

Here's an example from my mystery "Puzzling Ink."

The first of Blake Snyder's fifteen beats is the opening image. This is how it looks in my outline:

> *Quinn finishing crossword. Diner opens late because of festival. Cupcakes. OCD.*

This is how it reads when I flesh it out a bit more in my synopsis:

> *Opens with Quinn finishing up a crossword. Dad asks, "Doing one or making one?" Quinn tells Mom the diner opens late today because of the festival so she can help her carry the Cumin*

Cupcakes to Music Teacher's Assoc booth at 4th of July festival. Quinn is walking around the festival and finds herself not listening to conversation because she's silently counting red shirts [or flag shirts, or men wearing socks and sandals, etc]. She's subconsciously looking for patterns to control her world. When she helps her mom put down the cupcakes on the table at the booth, she comes back and rearranges them so they're in better order. Mom likes red frosted one, then white, then blue, over and over. Quinn wants all the red together, all white, all blue. Quinn counts and organizes things as her OCD manifestation.

And here are the first three pages of the manuscript I sent my editor. You can see it changed from a Fourth of July festival to a generic town festival.

The perfection of a pristine crossword puzzle grid always made Quinn Carr's pleasure center buzz. Like being touched by the hands of a lover, but better. Not like she'd felt that in a while, but she had a vague memory.

The puzzle was orderly. Symmetrical. No chaos. No mess. No negotiation. Only one correct answer.

A puzzle grid never looked at you funny when you agonized over some marketing sociopath who couldn't understand that "Pepper, Black" was worlds apart from "Black Pepper."

Crossword puzzles never judged you. Unlike the people who thought they knew all about you simply because you were in your thirties, had to move home with your parents, and needed—needed—to alphabetize their spices before you could continue creating the crossword puzzle for the local Chestnut Station Chronicle.

Quinn placed the turmeric next to the sesame seeds, not at all happy with the varying sizes of containers. Christmas was six months away. Maybe a new spice rack with matching jars would be a good present for her mom. But would that make her worry I was slipping? I could say it wasn't about me at all. Just trying to bring out her inner Julia Child.

And Georgeanne, Quinn's mom, definitely needed to get in touch with her inner Julia Child. Or Betty Crocker. Or even that Gorton's fisherman. Someone—anyone—who could help with her culinary endeavors.

As if on cue, Georgeanne shoved a cupcake toward Quinn's face.

"Taste this. I'm experimenting with cumin."

"Gross." Quinn twisted away, returning to her laptop at the kitchen table.

Quinn's dad, Dan, intercepted the cupcake and took a big bite. He accepted the culinary abomination with the good cheer of someone who hadn't been subjected to it for thirty-some years. Quinn admired her dad's skill at diplomacy. Was it possible he actually liked his wife's cooking? The world will never know.

"Hm." He chewed thoughtfully, frowning slightly. "The cumin is interesting, but what kind of frosting is that?"

Georgeanne beamed. "The white frosting is miso and the red is smoked paprika."

"You've done it again, Georgie." Dan polished off the cupcake then gave Quinn a kiss on the top of her head. "Solving a crossword or making one?"

"Making one."

"What's the theme?"

"Over. Like overshadow, overactive, overcharge, overexpose."

Georgeanne cocked her head. "Not Chestnut Days?"

"That ran a couple days ago. You're overanalyzing."

"Just overreacted. Aren't you going to be late for work?"

"Overexcited to get me out of here?"

"Trying to overcome my separation anxiety from my favorite child."

"Only child, but point well-taken. Jake's not opening the diner until after the parade. Nobody will be in before that." Quinn gestured toward the cupcakes. "I can help carry those to your booth if you want."

"I'm overwhelmed with joy for the offer." Georgeanne dipped a rubber scraper into the bowl of red frosting. "I need to finish these first, though. Eat some breakfast, Dan. I already made your oatmeal."

Dan and Quinn exchanged a smile behind Georgeanne's back. For the eight thousand years they'd been married, Georgeanne had been making Dan oatmeal for breakfast. In the beginning it was normal oatmeal, like most people ate. But over the years, Georgeanne increasingly expressed her creativity through her cooking. These days, Dan's oatmeal was virtually unrecognizable, buried under layers of dried and fresh fruit, nuts, seeds, roasted chickpeas, dried basil and tarragon. The pièce de résistance, however, was the artfully arranged spoonful of dill pickle relish on top. This flourish was added after Georgeanne heard a Japanese chef extol the virtues of "eating with your eyes," something Quinn desperately wanted to learn, if it meant she needn't use her mouth.

Quinn had never once seen her father refuse to eat something Georgeanne prepared, or even grimace in the slightest. Quinn tried to emulate him as much as possible because Georgeanne was the sweetest, kindest, best mother on the planet, but more often than she wanted, a wrinkled nose and a "gross" escaped her lips. Luckily Georgeanne was the sweetest, kindest, best mother on the planet, and such comments slid right off her like she was coated in Teflon.

Dan scooped a spoon into his hearty bowl of oatmeal and offered it to Quinn.

"No thanks, Dad. I already ate." Since Quinn had boomeranged back home a few weeks back, she'd learned to set an early alarm and make some toast and eggs before Georgeanne padded into the kitchen to begin her culinary calamities. Now that she had to be at the diner before seven, she had an excuse and it wasn't even awkward anymore.

In the outline I wanted to make sure to hit on four things: Quinn creates crossword puzzles; she also has a job at the diner; her mom's cupcakes; and Quinn's OCD, all of which are important to the story, and, in fact, the entire series.

The synopsis fleshes it out a bit. Those aren't just any cupcakes, they're ridiculous Cumin Cupcakes. Quinn walks around the festival where the reader sees her OCD.

Then the final version actually reads like a book, with details, description, setting, humor, and all the other goodies.

Small, medium, large. Outline, synopsis, manuscript.

You can see how I use my outline to start gathering the bones of my skeleton and put them in place. The synopsis joins them together and makes sure nothing falls off. Then the first draft of the manuscript puts a layer of skin over it all. The editing layers on the clothes, make-up, and hair. The polishing determines the style of clothes, how much make-up, and the particular coif.

Back to the synopsis. The first one is going to be full of holes, no matter how many you've written in the past. It's full of holes because you don't quite know your story yet. But you're still going to write a complete synopsis from your outline.

When you've written to the end of it, it will be around eight or ten pages. You're going to stop and read the synopsis you just wrote straight through, from beginning to end. You won't be editing or making any changes at all, but rather jotting notes of everything that needs research (no matter how small), or brainstorming to strengthen boring or clichéd parts. You'll also answer any questions that come up as you're reading.

- *How does small claims court work?*
- *Which disguises could she wear?*
- *Why would she be downtown at night?*
- *What's a funnier/spookier/less obvious way for him to get to that house?*

You'll have a million questions, leading to ways you can deepen your story. The more you know about the answers to all of them, the more it can inform your writing, and the quicker your draft will take shape.

For example, in "Fiction Can Be Murder" I was researching potential cars for Charlee to drive. I read some reviews of one that said the cup holders were huge. So, of course, I knew that was the car for her. I also knew at some point, she'd put a cup of her beloved coffee in there that would go flying out.

Don't fall down the rabbit hole of research, though. Get what you need then get out. You only have one week for the outline AND the synopsis.

Maybe you find out that small claims court has an arcane

rule that can become a clue or plot point. Maybe the disguise your character chooses should make her look just like the small claims court clerk, or to help her blend into the downtown festival being held that night.

Your research will *inform* your writing. Research is not to be used as an info dump to clobber your readers over the head about how small claims court works. Yawn.

After you do your research, then you're going to go back with that new information and fill in more details in your synopsis. You don't need to add them to your outline because that document has served its purpose now.

I've learned to think of my outline as my first draft, the synopsis as my second draft, and the first complete manuscript as my third draft.

As I'm considering each step in my outline, because I write mysteries, I'm also making a list of my clues and red herrings. I have all the information about my innocent suspects, too. I know who they are, what lies they've told, what truths they're telling, how all their lives intersect. I've added it all to my synopsis.

Lather, rinse, and repeat until your allotted time is up.

Speaking of allotted time ... if I were going to deviate from my eight-week schedule, this is where I'd do it. I think it's extremely important to get as much information as you can into the first drafts, whether it's during the outline phase or synopsis.

The more you pour into your outline, the more complete your synopsis will be, and the more questions you answer in your synopsis, the quicker and easier your complete draft will go.

When I'm done with my synopsis, it usually ends up being between twenty and thirty pages. At some point, though, I simply must set it aside to start writing because every time I read it, I think of new things to add: new layers, ideas, dialogue, what ifs, twists. Even when I allow myself extra time, I still put a deadline on it.

I can see you getting worried that you're not capturing all these new layers, ideas, dialogue, what ifs, and twists. But don't. No, you're not technically capturing them by writing them into your synopsis, but because your writing process is so condensed, all the good ideas will remain in the front of your brain. If they truly are good ideas, you'll see them in your draft. Trust those little gray cells. It's another reason to write faster.

I reserve an hour or so at the end of my outline/synopsis week to place all the events from the story on a timeline.

This serves two purposes. It gives me a checklist of scenes so I can make sure I've written them all, and it verifies that my timeline works.

Have you ever read a book and thought, "This person has 359 hours in every day!" or, "Wait. I thought weekends only had two days."

I love CalendarLabs.com and WorksheetWorks.com. Those are free websites where you can download all kinds of calendars. I have some calendar templates I use for the time management stuff, which we'll talk about later, but I also use my "Outlining Timeline" to make sure the plot works. It's one page for each day. (Downloadable PDF from BeckyClark-Books.com under the "Stuff I Teach" tab.)

It's easy to lose track of the timeline of your story when you're deep into it. So I like to make sure everything works from a bird's eye view before I start my draft.

The action in my books usually takes place in a fairly tight timeline, maybe a week or two from start to finish, so I plot all the action on my outlining timeline. I simply print out however many pages I need to cover the scope of the plot.

It's a very helpful snapshot of the action. It kept me from screwing up when my protagonist was supposed to be at work and when her day off was. That would have been a mess for me to untangle.

If your story is more epic in scope and takes place over

years, then you can do the same thing with a quarterly or yearly calendar.

I keep a folder on my desktop with blanks of all the calendars I like to use so I never have to go searching for them. I've labeled it, oh-so-cleverly, "blank calendars."

When I'm ready to start writing the draft, my synopsis and my timeline are next to me. The synopsis tells me what scene I'm supposed to be writing. The timeline makes sure everything is in the right order and serves as a double check that I didn't forget anything.

At the end of each of my writing sessions, I cross off the paragraphs of my synopsis that I completed. On my timeline, I put a checkmark next to each piece I accounted for in my writing.

If I've forgotten to put something in my manuscript after all that, it can only be because I've been kidnapped by my muse and deprogrammed.

Of course, if I take a little detour from my synopsis and timeline—which is perfectly fine—skipping down the path to Cinderella's castle when I originally intended to follow Hansel and Gretel to the house of candy, I have to make sure I've accounted for that time. If I've decided to stay at the ball until midnight to meet Prince Charming, then I can't have the next scene with me eating dinner before the ball. Nor could I have an earlier scene where I'd already met Prince Charming. I should see all of that quite clearly on the timeline.

If I reorganize some things and decide it really is a good idea to step off the path I've already made for my story, then great … rejigger and move along. But if it's not, then I can rewind and get back on my original path.

Or maybe it IS a good idea to go to Cinderella's ball, but not right now. I can check my timeline and see when I have some free time to meet my prince. Maybe three chapters from now would be better. I can note that on my timeline, then make a note on my synopsis to add the scene at the ball.

Your timeline should work hand-in-hand with your synopsis.

No synopsis is chiseled on stone tablets and carried around by Moses, though. Each pass you make through your synopsis clarifies the flow of your story and fleshes it out. I often write long passages of dialogue in the synopsis or funny bits and images that I don't want to forget. It always feels a bit like cheating when I get to copy and paste right into my manuscript. It's so exciting to see that word count jump up!

And speaking of word count ...

25

HOW TO WRITE FASTER

IT SOUNDS WOO-WOO, BUT YOU HAVE TO BELIEVE YOU CAN write faster and better. Until somebody broke the 4-minute mile, nobody believed it could be done. Now everyone but me is breaking it. But you also can't rush out and run a marathon simply because you believe you can. You have to work up to it. Get some systems in place for training and build those muscles and habits.

The other thing you must believe is that you're not twelve years old. (Unless you, dear reader, actually are twelve years old. Then carry on being twelve and writing those novels. You rock!) But if you're not twelve, turn off your phone and social media. There's nothing so important it can't wait until you're done with your writing for the day. And if there is some emergency, trust that other people can handle it.

But if you can't let go of the what-ifs, list all the things you *think* might happen while you're unavailable. Then examine your list with a hyper-critical eye. Are any of those things *really* likely to happen? Yes, there will be hiccups, and no, you can't plan for every little one, but know other people can and will help if there's some true emergency during your writing time. And in just one short hour you can check to see if any terrible emergency happened that was made worse because you were the only person on earth who could possibly have handled it.

Some people can work in short bursts of time. I'm not one of them. I like longer blocks of time to write, but maybe that's just because I *have* longer blocks of time to write.

During those short times when you're waiting for an appointment, or you're on a walk, or stuck in traffic, you can still be productive. I like to use those times and the early morning hours for brainstorming. I pick a topic, whether it's a plot hole, or how to get a character from here to there, or blocking a fight scene, or filling my "word bank" for thematic words and phrases I want to be sure to use. Then when you ARE ready to write, you're ahead of the game.

Let's talk for a minute about word banks.

When you have a theme or setting important to your story, you can do this very cool subliminal thing where your word choice slyly reminds your reader about it.

If one of your characters is Japanese, you're going to want to describe her eyes the color of jade; or see her going through a gate *as imposing as a Shinto shrine*, or trying on a dress *as tight as a kimono*, or slicing a loaf of bread with a knife *the size of a Samurai sword*.

Or if your book involves a marching band. Even when the characters aren't performing, they're *walking with precision*, or they're in *tight formation*, the anger in her voice is *percussive*.

If you want to show that your character is tender-hearted without having to say it all the time, curate a list of words that evoke puppies or kittens or comfort food or … whatever you have in mind to evoke that sort of feeling in your reader.

Then withdraw from your word bank during your editing and polishing phase, to subliminally remind your reader that you're in the world of marching band, or Japan, or outer space, or whatever.

It's very effective. You don't need to be heavy-handed about it, but these lists will serve you well. And you can create them in ten-minute brainstorming sessions. It is a super-productive use of your time, especially when you write a series and can refer to them over and over again. You can also use them to develop your titles. Double duty!

Back to writing fast.

The speed of your writing helps with your motivation for writing. There's a direct correlation. If it took two years to write a manuscript, I'd get sick of it. Writing a draft in two months is much more fun and energizing. Plus, you get the added benefit of having all the information fresh in your mind which makes the writing faster and easier. You're not having to look things up, you're not having to remind yourself what happened in earlier chapters or who these characters are.

You will write faster when you're excited about your book overall, and specifically the scene you're writing. I have the most trouble and slowest speeds when I haven't fully fleshed out, and therefore don't understand, the blocking of the action or the motivation for what's to happen.

Do not edit as you go, as tempting as it is.

Read over that sentence 7,362 times if you have to. I'll wait.

Editing as you go is a *huge* waste of time.

First of all, writing and editing use different parts of your brain and when you move from one to the other in an attempt to multi-task (which nobody can do), you won't do either of them well and you'll tire faster.

Second, it allows your inner editor to get all up in your business and put the kibosh on any creative momentum you get going.

And third, looking at it logically, why would you spend time polishing up a sentence, paragraph, or chapter that might get axed or relocated? Save your time and energy until you know your story is solid. Then, when the draft is complete, polish it up and make it shine.

To break you of the habit of editing as you go, when you're writing, close your eyes, turn off your monitor, or drape a towel over your screen. When you stop worrying about perfection and looking backward at what you've already completed, your fingers can really fly. Neurosurgeons need to be perfect; writers need to write.

If you're worried that your typing will be full of typos if you don't look, then I give you permission to unfocus your eyes and look back every once in awhile to make sure your fingers haven't djogyrf pmr ;ryyrt pm yjr lrunpstf, er … shifted one letter over on the keyboard.

Once you see how fast your words can fly on to the page, it won't take long to break yourself of that habit. With a tiny bit of self-control, you'll be able to ratchet up your daily word count, knowing you'll be making them better in just a few short weeks.

If not editing as you go is new to you, feel free to begin with short five-minute sprints and work your way up to longer writing sessions. If you're in the habit of fiddling with every word until it's "perfect" before you go on, you will need some time to retrain yourself. However long your writing sessions are, though, you *must* track your progress.

Don't fool yourself that you can write for a five-minute sprint, multiply it by twelve and get an accurate words-per-hour number. Only writing for a focused hour will get you an accurate words-per-hour number. And tracking many focused hours of writing will get you your average words per hour … a number you can always bank on. You will be able to state with confidence—to yourself or an editor—how fast you can consistently write, thereby knowing exactly how many days it will take to get a manuscript finished.

The other problem with editing as you go is that you don't see—and therefore won't learn from—your specific writing bugaboos. As you're barreling through your manuscript, tearing up the words, leaving a literary wake behind you, your foibles become obvious—your overuse of certain words, your default sentence structure, how many times your character laughs/shrugs/glances/rolls her eyes.

The more you see your bad habits, the more obvious they become, so the less you do it, and the better your writing gets.

When you type regularly for your hour(s) per day, and practice doing so without looking, you're automatically going to get faster and more accurate. Because that's what practice does.

Now, if you're a bad typist, you might need to add extra time to your eight weeks, but I bet you'll find you get better the more you type. Some of my friends have invested the time and money in dictation software or even a personal assistant to type what they dictate.

Dictation software like Dragon Dictate or even just the plain 'ol voice-to-text in Word can save your wrists, arms and hands. Once it's set up on your computer and in Word, it's just a push of a button to start dictating.

There's a learning curve, though, so I'd suggest before trying it on a manuscript, you practice in other parts of your life. Use it to make your grocery lists, unimportant emails, blog posts, texts, your annual Christmas letter, or your journal entries. Then, when it's more second nature, try it on a manuscript. I've heard that you should type when you're feeling your way through a scene, and dictate when you know what you want to say.

Professional typists pound out around 75 words per minute. The average person speaks 130-150 words per minute. Wouldn't it be cool to dictate an entire book in six or eight hours? However, if you like to write in public that could be kind of awkward. "Um, excuse me, ma'am ... who are you talking to? And did you just confess to multiple murders?"

Putting on my mathologist hat, that means if you type flat-out nonstop at professional typist speed for an hour, that would be 4500 words per hour. If you dictate for an hour, even at the low end, that's 7800 words per hour. My highest organic word counts (when there's no copying and pasting from my synopsis) are only in the 1400 range, and I consider that an excellent hour of writing. If it jumped to 7000 with dictation and I could consistently keep it up there, I'd ... well, I don't know what I'd do, but it would probably involve at least one cartoon happy dance. Maybe confetti. No, not confetti. I'd have to stop and vacuum then. But I'd toss virtual confetti, and tons of it.

Again, make your system and all your tools work for you. But maybe not in public.

When you write exclusively for a set period of time, whether twenty minutes or an hour, you are training your brain to get into that writing zone on command. No distractions, no editing. Just forward momentum on your story. Words, words, words, glorious words.

I talked about the magic of placeholder words earlier, but it bears repeating because they are so very useful.

Don't agonize over the perfect word when you're drafting. If that perfect word isn't there for you immediately, use a placeholder word as often as you need to. I put boring adjectives in brackets while I type. My manuscripts are full of [nice] [things], [pretty] [flowers], and [good] [food]. And unless I really know the description of something, I don't write it. I'll just make a note that says "describe outfit" or "describe room, be sure to mention the worn spot in the carpet." That stuff gets fixed in editing.

In my draft of PUZZLING INK I have two words in brackets on page 2....

[describe Georgeanne]

After editing I have 116.

Georgeanne's dimples deepened as they did whenever she smiled, which was pretty much constantly. Quinn loved those dimples despite the fact they were not symmetrical. It was quite obvious that her mother's cheeks didn't match. When Quinn was young, she'd gently tilt Georgeanne's head so the dimples would cross the same imaginary line bisecting her face. As she got older she learned she could simply tilt her own head if she wanted symmetry in her mother. Quinn had read once that the attractiveness of a face was in direct proportion to how symmetrical it was, but she had scoffed. Everything about her mother was appealing. Except maybe when she shoved a Cumin Cupcake in your face.

There was no way when I was writing page two of this manuscript that I knew Georgeanne well enough to know that this was her "telling detail," even after my character study. Telling details are so much more compelling than description anyway. It doesn't matter what color her hair or eyes are. You learn her approximate age from context in the story. But those dimples! That's what you need to know about Georgeanne. And this passage serves double duty by telling the reader a bit about Quinn, too.

If I'd written a description of Georgeanne instead of those two words in the brackets, it might have garnered me 100 more words, but it would have wasted a ton of time. Ten minutes? That's almost 20% of my writing time in that hour. Even if it was just five minutes, that's still too much because not only would I lose that time, but I would have had to delete those words anyway. Georgeanne's description didn't come easy to me in this first book in the series, especially on page two. But in "Punning with Scissors," book two in the series, I'll be able to spew 100 words about her with no problem, since I know her so well now.

Dialogue is another thing you can write fast and clean up in editing. If you have a long scene with dialogue between two people, just let 'er rip. You don't need to bother with quotation marks or dialogue tags. Your fingers can race through their argument, or their clever chatter, or their dissecting of the clues, or when they try to persuade that reluctant secondary character to come along on the quest.

Then in editing, you'll make it clear to your reader who is talking. You'll also add in some thematic words from your word bank, some appropriate stage action, and fine, quotation marks if you want to be all conventional and stuff.

The point is, you already have that conversation living in your head so don't let anything slow you down from getting it on the page. If you've practiced with dictation, it works beautifully with dialogue.

26

GUESS WHAT IT'S TIME TO DO ....
WRITE!

Yep. Now you know what you're going to write and you have some tools to get it on the page fast. Time to sit down and DO IT!

But before you sit down to write, gather up everything you'll need.

- tracking calendar for stats
- synopsis
- timeline
- character pages
- sketches of settings
- and your timer, to set for one-hour increments. If you have no willpower, then don't use your phone as your timer. Use a kitchen timer and keep your phone away from you, turned off in a different room.

Read the section in your synopsis and timeline that you're going to write about. Visualize the stage action and blocking if it's a complicated scene with a lot of movement. Act out the conversations. Know what your setting looks, smells, and sounds like. Then when you put your fingers on your keyboard, you're off to the literary races.

Write nonstop for one hour, until your timer rings.

When your hour is up, on your tracking calendar, jot

down the date and how many words you just wrote for Hour One. This is how you'll track your progress every day, so it's all in one place.

Take a 5-minute stretch, or have a Dance Party, or eat a tangerine, or whatever.

Then do another hour.

At the end of *that* hour, write down your 2nd hour word count on your tracking calendar.

Do that for every hour you write. First, one hour is easier math. Second, you need to remember to stretch every hour. More than an hour without a short break becomes counter-productive and can lead to physical problems.

At the end of your writing day, calculate your average words per hour for the day.

Print out your day's writing.

Email your manuscript to yourself.

You can certainly do your writing in 20- or 30-minute sprints, with my caution that you remember to stretch every hour. However, if you reward yourself with a 10-minute break after only 20 minutes of writing, you are going to fritter away a ton of writing time.

I'd really like to encourage you to work up to a solid hour of focused writing. But whatever you decide to do, make the math easy! Don't do 34-minute writing sprints with a 3-minute break between each.

On your tracking calendar, make sure you have a system to differentiate between hour-long sessions and 20-minute sprints. Otherwise your math will be all screwed up.

The first couple of times you attempt this, I want you to go *overboard* on your stats and recording your progress. You need to know **when** and **why** and **how** and **where** you write faster and better, and when it's agonizing to get any words out. You'll want to do more of the better stuff, and less of the worse. But without record-keeping you won't know which is which.

Like anyone, I always want to get more words per hour so

I periodically re-read Rachel Aaron's book "2k to 10k-Writing Faster, Writing Better, and Writing More of What You Love," her journey about going from 2k to 10k words per day. I encourage you to read it too, and revisit it every so often.

There's another guy you might be interested in, too. ChrisFoxWrites.com. He has a Kindle book called "5000 Words Per Hour."

It would be great to write that many words per hour, but don't obsess over numbers. Don't get me wrong, it is marvelous to see those numbers consistently improve—which they will, the more you do this. But I do all this just fine and I think my personal best hour (without the benefit of copying and pasting a huge block from my synopsis into my manuscript) was around 1400 words. And that doesn't happen every hour. Or even every day.

You can write from dawn until midnight if you want. Have a free weekend with no obligations? Go for it! Maybe you'll hammer out 50,000 words. That would be awesome, but a pace like that can take its toll, physically and emotionally. Remember, you want your plan to be sustainable for the long haul.

BUT, you do need to know what you're capable of AND your limits. So by all means, TRY for those 10,000 word days and see what happens. And CAPITALIZE random WORDS for EMPHASIS.

With concentrated writing, you're also practicing no editing—so very important—but also, and trust me on this, the *need* for editing lessens the more you do this. Your words come faster and they get better with every session of focused writing you get under your belt. I know you don't believe me, especially if you are in the habit of editing as you go, but that's why I want you to track your progress. Prove it to yourself, or prove it to me. But until you have some data, you'll never know.

As you get faster, your words will get better. Neuroscience, baby. It's what's for dinner.

One thing that helps me write faster is to check my synopsis and timeline for the scene(s) I need to write that day, before I need to start writing. Then I go about my business: breakfast, shower, pulling weeds, cleaning the kitchen, exercise, whatever.

While I'm doing those brainless chores, I mentally block that scene in my head. I watch the movie unspool in my brain. Then when it's writing time—BLAMMO—it explodes from my fingers onto the page. If it's a funny scene, it comes out funnier. Scary scenes are scarier. If I had the courage to write sex scenes, I'd expect I'd need a cigarette and a nap after I finished writing.

I get faster as I tally up those daily hours, but only up to hour three or so. If I write for four hours, that last one is almost always slower. It's just a natural—for me, anyway—response to the physical and mental aspect of what I'm doing. I might still decide to write that fourth hour, but I don't beat myself up over my word count. Plus, it keeps me humble.

I write in the same location every day. I stand on a mini-trampoline at a treadmill desk. I know. Weird. But, when I belly up to it, I know it's time to work. I've creatively brainwashed myself.

By using my schedule every day, I know what I'm supposed to be doing at all times. When I see that clock ticking down before a writing session, I feel antsy to get started. If I was a cartoon dog, I'd start drooling. Right now, as I write this, I know my writing time is getting short and I'll have to move on to a different, less fun task, so I can feel myself speed up. It's bizarre and makes me think I should leave my brain to science.

Unlike me, you might use your desk for other stuff besides writing or publishing tasks so you may not have the same Pavlovian response as I do.

You might start drooling when you take your laptop to the park, or when you hear the first chords of your *Music To Write To* playlist, or catch a whiff of the match as you light your lavender candle. You need to find the thing that signals your brain that now is the time to write.

But I don't fool myself into thinking that everyone would be happy doing what I do. Same place every day? *Yuck!* Same time every day? *No possible way!* Standing on a trampoline? *That's ridiculous!*

And that's the beauty of this system. It's yours and yours alone. Test the things you can. Find your sweet spot. Make it work for you. It simply doesn't matter what works for other people. The only thing that matters is what works for you. But to know that, you need to be open to other ideas and experiment with them. We're all on our way up the mountain. Maybe you can hike for a while on a trail someone else has already cleared.

When I'm done writing for the day, I do all the math for my stats that day, print the day's pages, and place them in 3-ring binder WITHOUT LOOKING AT THEM. They're not perfect. I know that. But it's not time to worry about that yet.

Then I do something much more important. I attach my manuscript in an email to both of my email addresses. The subject line says the title and the date.

I should tell you that when I stop for lunch, I email my work to myself as well. In the subject line I put the title and the date but add "lunchtime" after it. I know that if I have another email for that date afterward, I can delete the lunchtime email.

Yes, thank you for asking, I *have* lost my work before. But not since implementing this incredibly simple system. Just recently I got spooked by a phishing hack attack on my computer, but I never worried about losing anything. It's excellent peace of mind.

I'm very analog. I love paper and pencil. Of course you can use an app or a spreadsheet to track your writing progress, but understand that every time you click something that's not your manuscript, you run the risk of getting distracted by the cyber world. And honestly? There's something very satisfying about paper and pencil tracking. It lives in the front pocket of my binder. I never lose it and can always refer to it, even without electricity.

Try it and see. Electronic doesn't necessarily mean better. Shall we fight? You can use your crashed computer as your weapon and I'll wield my mighty, mighty pencil.

I joke, but paper and pencil will never fail you. I read an article about a typewriter exhibit at the American Writers Museum in Chicago. A fifth grader exclaimed, "Wow! This is great. It's an instant printer!"

I feel the same way about paper and pencil. They never disappear in a power outage, they never require a login or password, and it never takes more than fifteen seconds to record your writing stats.

I don't trust that ephemeral Cloud, so every few days I hook up my external hard drive and back up everything on my computer too. It takes no time, and when—not if—your computer crashes, you won't be a quivering mess of writerly jelly we have to mold and prod back into shape.

I don't rely solely on an external drive because it, too, can fail. Your email probably won't. And *both* your emails certainly won't. If you only have one email account, consider setting up another at a different provider to dedicate to this. People mock the ancient AOL address I still have, but I've never had one minute of trouble with it. I figure the hackers have forgotten all about it. Shhh.

The next day, when I'm ready to get started, I'll read the next bit of my synopsis and story timeline, then a paragraph or two from yesterday's writing, set my timer, and off I go.

By the way, I try to stop writing in the middle of a sentence because it gets me right back into it faster. When you stop for the day at the end of a scene or chapter, the next day you're confronted with that dreaded blank screen. Even when you outline and have a plan to move forward, there's just something so psychologically painful about that blankness.

Maybe that's not an issue for you, but if it is, try stopping in the middle of a sentence and see what happens.

People ask me all the time why I print out my pages every day. I do it for two reasons. One, I edit better on paper. Two, even though I back up my digital work religiously, it makes me feel warm and cozy to have a hard copy. I'm kind of a Luddite at heart. Surprise!

Again, you do you.

27

RECORD-KEEPING

I HOPE BY NOW YOU UNDERSTAND THE IMPORTANCE I PLACE ON keeping track of everything.

The only way you're going to know what's working for you and what's not is by keeping meticulous track of *everything* each time you sit down for a writing session.

You won't have to do it forever, so don't get lazy and shirk this duty up front. Know that if you refuse to do your record-keeping, you definitely won't know how to get faster with your writing, where and when and how you work best, and whether you're on track with your eight-week process.

Write down EVERYTHING your first few times through the eight-week process. Of course, you'll want your basic stats on your Tracking Calendar, but you also need to know where you wrote and when, how you felt about it, things you'll do differently next session, what worked, what didn't. What were you afraid of? Did your fears come true? Was today's writing easier or harder than you expected? Why do you think that is? Were you distracted? Were you interrupted by outside forces? Write down *everything*.

But you're not going to consider any of these things until after your writing session is over. During your hour (or whatever amount of time you carved out), all you're going to do is outline, or draft, or edit your manuscript—wherever you are in the eight-week process.

At the end of each session, though, you're going to take five or ten minutes to debrief with yourself … in writing.

Get a spiral notebook or a fancy journal or just open another file on your computer dedicated to this. Write the date and time then commence journaling your thoughts.

Don't worry about complete sentences or think too hard about what you're saying, just dump what's left of your brain into this journal. A bulleted brainstorm list, or solid block of stream of consciousness works great. Jot down whatever comes to mind. What was hard? What was easy? What do you feel good about? What was distracting? Did you stick to your plan? Step off your path? Were you a whir of *in-the-writing-zone* activity? Anything and everything that comes to mind.

You will have experimented with *where* you write, so check in with yourself. Was it a mistake to write at the coffee shop? Did you get more words sitting at your desk than when you lounged on the couch? Did the study carrel at the library provide you with sufficient blinders so you could focus, or was it more like a claustrophobic deprivation chamber?

You will have experimented with *when* you write. Did you get more words when you wrote before work or late at night? 10:00 a.m. vs 2:00 p.m? When you concentrated for a full hour or when you did three 20-minute sprints? How was it when you tried to write on your lunch break at work?

You will have experimented with *how* you write. Are you still trying to edit as you go? (If so, KNOCK IT OFF!) Have you tried using the placeholder words? How's that going? Is your outline, synopsis, and timeline complete enough for you, or do you find yourself stuck about what to write next? Should you stop the drafting and revisit your outline to flesh it out more, or are your fingers flying through your draft because your synopsis is stellar?

How are you feeling about the whole process? Is there

guilt because you told your family you're unavailable for an hour? Were they more supportive than you expected? Are you tired from getting up earlier or staying up later than normal? How can you fix that? Are you gaining confidence as you write faster? Are you feeling anxious? Is it because this is something entirely new for you? Do you find it difficult to change your habits? Is your dog staring at you with sad, hungry eyes because you're not distracting yourself by getting a snack every three minutes?

Whatever you're feeling, no matter how ridiculous it may sound, write it down.

If you see a pattern or you're not happy with something obvious, change it. If you were twice as productive on your couch from 10pm-11pm than you were at 5am-6am at your desk, then quit writing at 5am at your desk!

But if you're working through feelings of guilt for taking an hour for yourself away from your family, then that might not be a quick fix for you. Just let it sit. Journal about your guilt or your anxiety or whatever you're feeling without trying to fix it. Act like Paul McCartney and let it be.

Then, at the end of your eight weeks, read through your journal and see where you are. Did the anxiety lessen? Why or why not? What is the source of it? What can you do to alleviate it? Did the guilt go away as you played with where and when you wrote? Did your family settle down and realize you deserve time to write every day? Did YOU realize you deserved it?

Here's some more of the woo-woo I claim to disavow, but writing is a very specific endeavor. It takes oodles of brain space, both emotionally and cognitively, and you might need to free some of that up so you can do what you love.

The first step, though, is figuring out where you are and what's helping and hindering you to get there.

That's the reason to pay attention to yourself and write it down. After the eight weeks, you may transform into an entirely different writer, simply by checking in with yourself every day.

Okay. Enough of that. Woo-woo. I hope like me, your chakra has been cleansed and your chi is fully involved in synergistic vibrations. Now I feel like eating something made of quinoa and metaphysics.

28

IT'S TIME FOR THE EDITING PHASE

Here is where you pull out your thesaurus and word bank lists. It's where you fix your typos, add description, emotion, theme, and replace those boring clichés and placeholder words with something vivid and perfect.

We each have our "writer's voice"—what makes my books sound like me and your books sound like you. But within our books we also have many voices. Again, even though you've done your character studies and you know that Gladys, the girlfriend of your protagonist, is from Alabama, she doesn't *sound* like she's from Alabama yet. Now, during your editing phase, is the time give her some good Southernisms to say, or show her making cheese grits, blue crabs, and pe-CAN pie for dinner. Or put her in her Crimson Tide football jersey to go to a formal affair.

This is your chance to sprinkle Gladys dust all over her appearances. Maybe it will even lead to another scene where she goes to a football game and ends up sitting in the middle of a bunch of Auburn fans. Oooh, maybe that's where she overhears some important clue, or sees something she shouldn't have. Or has a realization that maybe this football rivalry is just like what her boyfriend, the main character, is going through. Or maybe teamwork is your theme and here's another opportunity to show that.

You get the idea. You're deepening and layering, now that you know your story and characters better.

Now that you've finished your manuscript, do your math to see how much editing you'll need to do. Divide the total number of your manuscript pages into your total number of editing days available. Don't stop until you've done at least those required pages each day. You can always do more, of course, but never less. And just because you only wrote four days per week, it doesn't mean you can't edit seven days, or three. Make your schedule work for you.

Personally, I find this editing phase much less taxing on my widdle bwain so I can do a lot more of it. The writing phase is fun in that I finally get to tell my story, and there's huge accomplishment in that, but the editing feels more personal to me, where I get to sprinkle Becky dust on it. Like the difference between building a house and decorating it. You get to choose paint colors—maybe even mix your own— pick out the perfect appliances, carpet, furniture, and window coverings. It's exactly the same as every other house in the world in that it has a roof, floor, and walls, but it's completely different. Just like books all have covers, pages and words, but they're all unique, even within the same sub-sub-sub-genres.

Polishing your words, finding the perfect turn of phrase, drilling down to the precise telling detail in your descriptions … there's nothing more uniquely *you* than that! This is where you get to make sure your distinct voice is heard, the quality that makes your book yours and yours alone.

Back to the math.

The first draft of FOUL PLAY ON WORDS was 163 pages. Divided by 8 days (which is all I allowed myself, per my schedule) works out to 21 pages/day for editing.

$163 \div 8 = 21$

Always round up, people. Always round up. A little or a lot.

I rounded to 25 pages to give myself a buffer. I take those 25 paper pages out of my binder and gather up everything I need: thesaurus; emotional thesaurus; character pages; sketches of the town, or whatever setting I'm working on; and anything else I think I might need for that day's session. Don't spend your precious time looking for info. That's the other reason I love my binder. Everything is in one place.

I absolutely do more editing if I have time. I like having that buffer because some days the editing is very light and other days I'm writing extra scenes … and I don't always know where they'll end up in the timing of my editing. If I decide to add a whole new scene that takes me an hour, you can bet your sweet bippy I'm happy that I worked ahead.

Also, as far as organizing … my 3-ring binder has tabs and pockets for everything I need. My manuscript pages go in front, then there are tabs for my outline, characters, research, a place for editorial notes or comments from my beta readers, and marketing ideas.

We talked about those character pages earlier. I can't stress this enough. One page per character. And make it visual rather than long blocks of text describing them. One thing it took me way too long to do was alphabetize my character pages. (I know, right??) I wasted a lot of time flipping through looking for someone. I guess I originally thought that the characters with the most screen time should go before the secondary characters. But that's just dumb. Alphabetizing is the only logical way to go, especially when you consider that you probably already know everything about your main character anyway.

In the front cover pocket I keep things like the maps I sketched and scraps of paper with great metaphors or a joke I want to use, or anything that doesn't have a better place to go. Have I mentioned how much I love my binder?

I also keep a legal pad nearby as I'm editing where I keep

a running list of "facts" from the story that I know will come up later and I won't want to waste time searching for the verification. *The patio faces south. Her hotel room is 809. Duke (springer spaniel) came in first place.*

I try to note the page numbers where I dropped all the important clues. I list the names of very minor characters who don't quite warrant their own character page. Jot down everything you know you'll need that you don't want to search for later. Just a quick glance fills in those blanks for you when you want to confirm something. A huge part of editing is confirmation of facts and continuity.

The cleaner you make your draft, the easier you make it on your final editor. If it's the in-house editor at your publishing house, you free up time and space for them to go deeper into their editing process. If it's a freelance editor you're paying, all the clean-up you do ahead of time not only allows them to go deeper into your manuscript, but also saves you money.

Part of my editing is making sure my story timeline works, so here is where I pull out my timeline again and make sure everything is in there. If I added or deleted stuff, does it still work with my timeline?

Like I said, I edit mostly in pencil on the pages I printed out every day after my writing sessions. But if I have a scene to add or a long section of new text, then I type directly into the computer to save time. Be sure to scrutinize these sections during your polishing week because you're bound to have made typos and perhaps some continuity problems for yourself. By typing them in directly, you lose one chance at editing them so your other editors have to make up for it.

Part of the reason I love using my pencil is because I'm very visual. When I'm editing my manuscript, I'll remember writing in the margin something about small claims court or that festival and I can find my handwritten notes on the page much faster. I think many of us have a sense memory of where we wrote those words, whether we're conscious of it or not.

Conversely, to search for a particular passage on the computer means you need to know some exact and unique words to find it. Don't get me wrong ... that's very helpful and efficient sometimes, but only if you can conjure up that exact phrase.

I had that problem when editing this book. I wanted to add something to the section about multi-tasking, which I typed into the search bar with the hyphen. Problem was, in my draft, sometimes I typed it without the hyphen, sometimes I typed it with a space, sometimes I didn't, and sometimes, if you can believe it, I misspelled it altogether. It's not the most earth-shattering problem to have, but one that sucked up an annoying amount of time.

You could also use a different font color for your new scenes. Or bold the text you add. Again, whatever works for you to locate words and ideas quicker. You will devise your processes the first few times you do this eight-week system, revising them until they're perfect for you. All this might be overwhelming right now, but once you get into it, I guarantee you will make it your own and it will make perfect sense.

It's like driving a car. If you'd never done it before, it would be overwhelming to hear all the steps you need to go through just to back out of the driveway. But once you go through taking the key out of your purse or pocket, holding it the right way, placing it properly into the lock, sitting down, swinging your legs into the car ... blah, blah, blah ... it will require much less thinking.

When I'm through editing the whole manuscript, that's when I type my changes in. I don't do it as I go because sometimes I change something in Chapter 12 that affects Chapter 5. It's the same reason we don't edit while we write. It's two different processes, and wastes too much time.

As I'm typing my changes, it gives me another chance to polish a bit more, finding better words, funnier or more intriguing dialogue and description. Plus I find and fix mistakes I didn't see before (or new ones I've created with my new additions).

Because I build in extra time by editing more pages each day than the math dictates, I have plenty of time at the end.

When I'm done editing for the day, I write my editing stats on my tracking calendar. Total number of pages I got done, and pages per hour. In case I haven't stressed it enough, the stats are important for Future You. When you've written a few manuscripts this way, you'll have a pretty solid idea of how many words you can write every hour, and how many pages you can edit. So, at some point, when you've made this system your own, you're going to be über-confident when you look at a blank calendar and say, "Why yes, Dream Editor! Yes, I CAN get three books written this year!"

I also check off everything that's happened on my outlining timeline and make sure the timing is still correct. Again.

29

WEEK 8 IS THE FINAL POLISH

AFTER I'VE MADE ALL MY CHANGES AND DONE GOOD EDITING work in Weeks 6 and 7, mostly I get to sit and read through fairly quickly with just my polishing cloth at the ready.

This read-through is very valuable, so don't skip it. If you can let your manuscript sit for a few days before the read-through, that's even better. I made a mistake recently when I finished up my editing phase and the next day started right into my read-through. I still had yesterday's information in the front of my brain, so I kept having moments of panic thinking I said something twice, or didn't drop that clue soon enough, and what-have-you. If I'd let it rest for a couple of days, I could have seen it with fresher eyes and kept my blood pressure within the normal range.

When you sit and read straight through you can catch so many piddly continuity problems, see that you've used the same word too many times, realize that Chapter 9 would be better broken into two. You'll just find stuff that you don't see when you read over a longer period.

One thing that helps me is to import it to my Kindle so I'm not tempted to fiddle with word choice anymore, just a strict read-through.

There's no reason to fiddle with those words right now,

anyway. You've made it the best you can *at this moment* but rest assured, you will see this manuscript again. Before you send it off to an agent. After you get notes back from your beta readers. When your editor sends your galleys. You will definitely get a chance to polish it up a bit more.

Now, if I haven't done good editing work in Weeks 6 and 7, then Week 8 looks an awful lot like Weeks 6 and 7, only much harder because I have to do more words in half the time.

Pro tip — I went to a writer's retreat many years ago with a session led by Darcy Pattison. She taught me the concept of a Shrunken Manuscript that you might find useful on your editing journey, too. If there's some aspect of your manuscript you want to check—how much screen time a certain character gets, or if you've woven in your subplot tightly enough, or where you've dropped clues, or really, anything—then change the color of the type of the sections you want to check, then select the entire document and shrink it to 6-point type with quarter-inch margins and single spacing. You'll end up with not too many pages and can see at an easy glance anything you want to double check. You could even check ALL of these things … screen time for Gladys in green, screen time for Hubert in red, subplot A in yellow, subplot B in purple, clues in orange.

It's quite a nifty way to see the structure of your manuscript without getting bogged down in all the words. Seeing the forest instead of the trees, if you will.

There's a link in the Resources to Darcy's website where she talks more about the Shrunken Manuscript.

"OKAY, BECKY," I HEAR YOU SAY. "YOU'RE A GENIUS, IT'S obvious. Now I'm convinced I can theoretically outline, write, edit, and polish my novel in eight weeks. But how in the world am I going to find the time to do this??"

First, you're not going to "find the time." That's not a thing. Nobody ever finds time. People can only manage the time they're given.

You accomplish what you focus on. When you focused on learning to drive, what happened? You learned to drive and you, presumably, do it without thinking too hard about it now. If you focus on writing a manuscript in eight weeks, the same thing will happen … you'll figure out how to make the time to get it done. If you focus on becoming a full-time author, guess what will happen?

You accomplish what you focus on. If you focus on watching every episode of Game of Thrones, guess what you'll accomplish?

The trick is to actually focus on what needs to be focused on. Learning to use what little time you have more efficiently. Efficiency is a self-perpetuating cycle. You learn to tell your stories faster ... which allows you to write more stories ... which teaches you to write better and faster ... which sells more books ... so you gain more confidence ... to tell more stories.....

Just like with the outlining piece, I'll show you my planning tools (also downloadable from BeckyClarkBooks.com), but keep in mind everyone is different. We all have different amounts of time available to us, different family situations, different skills and problems, different internal clocks. Pick and choose the ideas that will work with YOUR life and that will solve YOUR problems.

Everyone needs a plan to fit in everything they want to do every day, week, month, and year. Just like with outlining, there are many different paths to the same destination.

Let's try to find the right one for you.

30

TIME MANAGEMENT IS SIMPLE BUT NOT EASY

ALL YOU HAVE TO DO IS WRITE DOWN WHAT NEEDS TO BE DONE, then plug it into the time you have available to do it. Simple.

Saying we can manage time, however, implies we have control over how it behaves. But I'm sure I don't have to tell you that it's easier to control a twenty-pound bag of chocolate pudding. Or a mob of 13-year-old girls at a Justin Bieber concert. Or you at a table with free books.

"Time management" is a stupid term. How do you manage something that exists in the same way no matter what we do? All we can manage are our activities. But "activity management" sounds even stupider.

The annoyance you feel when you have to wait in line at the post office, or in the carpool lane at the school, or at the deli counter, or really, anywhere, has nothing to do with the time you have. The problem is with your brain telegraphing —often loudly—that you simply don't have enough time. Change your mindset. Personally, I love to wait in line because I always have a notebook or my Kindle or a magazine with me. Guilt-free reading! Fill your pocket notebook with words for your word bank. Sketch out the stage action for that fight scene in Chapter 12. Text yourself practice loglines for your story. Mull over possible subplots, or themes, or character names, or … well, you get the idea.

A lot of what we think of as *writing* is really *thinking*. So when you're given the gift of unexpected time in the form of long lines or traffic jams or boring meetings, use it to your advantage.

You will always have obstacles in your quest to wrangle your allotted 24 hours, whether it's internal (you) or external (them). But the solution always lies within you, Grasshopper.

These time management ideas may seem rigid, but just like your outline, schedules should be fluid enough to allow for interruptions and other obstacles. As long as you don't stray too far from your schedule, it will take care of you and create some balance back in your life, allowing you to do everything your little heart desires.

My biggest time management problem is not wanting to move on to my next task. Once in a while that's okay, finishing that last chapter instead of answering email, for instance. But eventually that email will end up strangling me, making it that much harder to wrangle the next day. And three days of that? Practically insurmountable. So, if I make the choice—and it's always a choice—to ignore the schedule I so carefully crafted for myself, I know I'm screwing up my productivity. I'll have to work on the weekend to make up for it, butting into my Becky Time and making me cranky. It's rarely worth it. Just ask my husband.

We've been talking so far about your writing life, but I recognize that you have a full and rich personal life as well. Significant others to hang out with, children to raise, corporate ladders to climb, books to read, movies to watch, parties to attend, pubs to crawl, houses to clean, laundry to wash, canvases to paint, gardens to plant, lawns to mow … there are a million fun and tedious activities constantly vying for your attention.

Your ultimate goal here is to marry efficiency with quality of life, whatever that looks like for you.

If your efficiency is buried under bad habits, don't worry. Bad habits can be unlearned and replaced with better ones. My guess is, since you're reading this, you're happy (or at least open) to do just that.

But really? The only person who likes change is a wet baby.

Give yourself at least thirty days to change and create new habits. Habits—good or bad—create neural pathways in the brain. Have you ever wondered why elderly people can remember what happened to them in third grade, but not what they had for breakfast? It's because of these neural pathways. They've had eighty years to travel back and forth to third grade, but only a few hours back to breakfast. The path to their past is as well-trod as a shortcut through a college campus.

Just because your bad habit path is well-trod, though, doesn't mean you can't get back on the sidewalk. It doesn't take willpower to change those bad habits; it takes persistence. Your job is to create an opening for change to waltz in.

Don't think of your life as just work and home. Everyone's work life is different, but your home life should include *physical health* (sleep, exercise, proper diet, regular medical/dental check-ups); *hanging out with people you love*; and *'filling your cup.'* I talk about filling your cup a lot because it's so very important. It's whatever transports you to a place of pure joy. I love live theatre so I make sure I set aside money and time for those forays into the world of Broadway. But other people fill their cup with nature, or volunteering, or baking, or alone time, or reading, or longs talks with their bestie … filling your cup can involve literally anything that makes you happy.

Now it might seem counter-intuitive to *add* something to your day if you're struggling with your schedule, but doing something you love energizes you in a million different ways. It makes you a better person, spouse, parent, employee. It's like when they tell you on the airplane to put on your own mask first.

Again, it might seem counter-intuitive, but if you're feeling overwhelmed or overworked, you should absolutely take a 'mental health day' and step away from your work. You don't have to have that 100% mindset we talked about earlier.

"Work" in this context encompasses both the job that pays your salary AND the writing work that you create for yourself. Nobody is forcing you to write a novel … but you want to. It fills your cup. Even though it's a joy, for our purposes, let's consider it work. (And if you've ever written one, you're probably laughing hysterically that anyone *wouldn't* consider it work!)

When you take a mental health day and get a change of environment, you'll be rested, energized, and more productive. It doesn't have to be much: taking a walk, going to a museum, indulging in a long bath, having lunch with a friend, watching a movie. A rewarding personal life makes it easier to tolerate frustrations at work and in the world at large.

Just like in the writing process we've been talking about, you're going to have to be honest with yourself about your time management saboteurs. Perfectionism? Procrastination? Social media? Whatever your personal bug-a-boo is. Because even if you take all this to heart and change your bad habits, they will eventually creep back in unless you're diligent. Have you ever been on a diet and said, "Carbs will never pass these lips again"? Or have you ever had a wicked hangover and vowed never to drink again? Or received a speeding ticket that made you promise to drive five miles under the speed limit forever and ever, world without end? How'd that work out for you? Just be aware and constantly check in with yourself.

There's a never-ending barrage of data jabbing at you every day, maybe every minute. Email, social media, phone calls, texts, Netflix, podcasts, snail mail, real live people, print books, audiobooks, ebooks, television, newspapers, magazines, lions, and tigers, and bears. Oh my!

It all needs to be sorted. Which is valuable and which is not? Which provides joy and which is just noise? Which is helpful to your goals and which is harmful?

Each day, each moment, is different. Just like a hospital ER, you need to learn the concept of triage. Most important first.

Understand, though, that your definition of "important" will ebb and flow, swell and shrink, loom and hide constantly, which is why you must also learn to trust and rely on your schedule. It can be very stressful to bump something low on your list of priorities that someone else thinks is desperately important. But if you allow others to determine what's important to you, then you're always going to be pulled in directions away from your goals.

For instance, I had to re-evaluate how I used Facebook. There was a time when I could scroll through my feed and see posts from most everyone I wanted every day. But time marched on. My list grew unwieldy. Facebook changed their algorithms, making it impossible to see what I wanted to see, instead choosing posts (and ads) for me. Guess what? They chose poorly. So now, I've created a group, Becky's Book Buddies, for direct, easy interaction with my readers. I respond to messages and notifications from people on my friend list, and, if I have time, I scroll for a set amount of time through my feed, usually only five or ten minutes. This has saved my sanity and my schedule.

Keep the helpful. Drop the harmful. Trust the plan you've made. It will get easier.

31

LET'S GET PRACTICAL

I've been The Queen of Time Management for a long time now—teaching workshops since the early 1990s and in managing my real life—and I'm going to offer you ideas and strategies that always work for me, regardless of how busy I am or what I'm focused on.

This is an exercise I have everyone in my workshops complete. It's very eye-opening for most people. You can revisit it and redo it as often as you want, certainly whenever there's a change in your circumstances.

On a sheet of paper, I want you to take a couple of minutes and jot down everything you want to do in all aspects of your life *regardless of time or money*. Write that novel. Spend more time with your kids. Visit Antarctica. Learn to crochet. Build a log house and live off the grid. This is just for you, so really do this. Dream big. Keep it handy because you'll need it later.

Are you done? Okay, fine. Five more minutes.

Everything on this list is WHY you want to manage your time better. Set it aside for now. Next, download a copy of the "Weekly Planner With Times" chart from BeckyClark-Books.com.

	MONDAY	TUESDAY	WEDNESDAY	THURSDAY	FRIDAY	SATURDAY	SUNDAY
4:00am							
5:00am							
6:00am							
7:00am							
8:00am							
9:00am							
10:00am							
11:00am							
12:00pm							
1:00pm							
2:00pm							
3:00pm							
4:00pm							
5:00pm							
6:00pm							
7:00pm							
8:00pm							
9:00pm							
10:00pm							
11:00pm							
12:00am							
1:00am							
2:00am							
3:00am							

YOU'LL SEE THIS TIMELINE COVERS TWENTY-FOUR HOURS.

The timeline I used in the past for this exercise only went from 5am to 8pm. I liked using it because it was a good reminder for people to start winding down their day. Not that I wanted everyone in bed by 8 p.m., although, wouldn't that be nice?

I realized there were plenty of people who work odd hours, or who have a newborn in the house, or are just naturally night owls. Regardless of your schedule, though, I really do want you to be winding down your day at a reasonable time… whatever that looks like for you.

So many health problems could be avoided if we just got enough shuteye. Sleep deprivation is seen as a status symbol these days; a badge of honor as to your dedication and work ethic. However it's simply unhealthy to get less than seven or eight hours per night.

I know a lot of you are staring loudly at me right now because there's no possible way you're ever going to get a solid seven hours of sleep. If you got five restless hours you'd be ecstatic. And I get that, really I do. Insomnia is a huge problem for which I have no answer.

But that's not what I'm talking about. I'm talking about those people who could sleep just fine if they'd only shut off Netflix, or close their book, or unplug the game console.

32

THE ALL-IMPORTANT SCHEDULING ACTIVITY

Now that we understand each other, let's do some work on this weekly timeline. Do this exercise as your schedule really is, not as you wish it was, or how you think it should be. How it really is, warts and all. If Monday – Friday is exactly the same or if every day is wildly different, so be it. This is your life and it's marvelous.

For those of you who work for yourselves and don't have a boss telling you when to do things, you'll want to keep track of an actual week in your life. Write down *exactly* what you did during these hours and then come back here and do this scheduling exercise. It will help you really see where your time goes every day, which is often not at all what you expected.

You may want to track an actual week in your life even if you don't work for yourself. It would help you prove to your boss that you really do get interrupted forty-seven gajillion times during the day so you deserve an assistant.

Or track your time away from the office so you can figure out exactly where you might see places where you're wasting time that could be used for writing.

Go old school for this tracking. You want a small notebook

with pen attached that you can carry with you. Start at the top of the page as soon as you get out of bed ….

5:03am - 5:22 fed the dog, made coffee

5:22 - 5:57 Facebook

5:57 – 6:55 treadmill and stretching

Etc. Every minute accounted for until you rest your head on the pillow again.

Tracking one day is good. Three is better. A full week tells you everything you'll ever want to know, plus allows for the weird variations of your life.

Then analyze your data. What did you do that had to be done? What did you do that could have been curtailed? What can you cut out of your schedule completely?

I don't know the right answers for you. But if you're honest with yourself, you'll see many places where you can use your time differently if you're serious about reshifting your priorities to get more writing done.

Back to the timeline.

This works really great if you have colored pencils, crayons, or markers, in a bunch of different colors. If not, no worries. Plain 'ol pencils work just fine. It helps to label the blocks of time as you shade them in, so you remember what they represent.

• If you have a job outside the house, shade in the hours you work and commute, if you drive. If you take public transportation, you're ahead of the time management game. Don't think that your efficiency problem has to do with having a day job, by the way. Lots of people report getting more writing done while they had a full-time job because they were forced to focus harder. When you know your only times to write are while waiting for meetings to start, or during your commute, or at lunch, or before work, or late at night … then that's when you write. No dilly-dallying.

• If you work at home at a job with a boss dictating the hours you work, shade in those hours.

• If you work at home and you're your own boss, it's trickier. Those of us who work at home can "work" all the time and for some of us, "work" is really fun so it doesn't seem like "work." We get to spend a lot of time doing jobs we love. But even those of us who love our jobs still spend a lot of time doing what we HAVE to do versus what we'd LIKE to do. So if you work at home without a boss demanding regular hours, then don't shade in anything for your "workday." Those hours will be filled with your to-do list activities that we'll get to later, or with your real-life activities you just tracked for a week. That said, if you've been working for yourself for a long time, feel free to shade in the appropriate number of hours for your workday. Note I said *appropriate*. If you're having time management problems, perhaps you need to rethink your approach to your workday. Have you fallen into some bad habits over the years? Are you filling time with *busy work* instead of *real work*?

The problem, as one of my workshop participants told me, is that "if all your time is unclaimed, then there are no boundaries or clarity to your day and you get trapped in cycles of indecision."

If that sounds like you, then definitely do the "tracking your real week" exercise.

If your quest is to be a career author, then maybe you need to study how you're actually spending your time AND fill out an "aspirational" work day.

For me, I can tell you that I allow four hours for writing and two-and-a-half hours for marketing and other business-related activities, every weekday except Wednesday. That's Becky Day when I have lunch with friends, go to the dentist, take care of household chores. And I don't work on weekends.

Except when I do.

Like I said, schedules are fluid, stretching and shrinking to encompass what needs to be done.

But all that white space is both a blessing and a curse. So, after you've tracked your real life, block similar chores together, and add up those times. When you see where your time HAS BEEN going, you can better tweak it to where you WANT IT TO GO in the future. Then, shade in an aspirational work day.

• Next, shade in one hour/day for exercise— that's right, all seven days. It doesn't have to be the same time every day. If you take a yoga class on Thursday night, go to kickboxing Tuesday morning, lift weights in your basement twice a week after work, and walk on the treadmill every morning, then shade in those times. If you don't exercise regularly right now, just shade in one hour, ideally the first thing in morning. I'm a good little exerciser, but if I don't do it first thing, it doesn't get done. And it's such a great way to start your day. It gives you a real boost all day and you know, without me having to bash you over the head, that it's the healthy thing to do. The important thing is to do it; don't worry about when. And yes, it's non-negotiable. You'll hate me for a while, but then you'll love me. No, really.

I'm a real cheerleader for regular exercise, especially strength training. In January 2017 I had a benign tumor removed from inside my spinal column that had—over the course of many years, apparently—slowly pushed my spinal cord from a straight "I" into a bulgy "D" (I know!!) in January 2017. It was a weird, unwelcome surprise, but because of the strength in my legs, core, and arms, relearning to walk, sit, stand, and use stairs was much easier. You just never know when you'll get a curveball thrown directly at you so it's better to be ready for it. So when I say "please exercise," it's not because I care how you look in a swimsuit. It's because this quality of life issue only gets more important as we get older. I watched, helpless, as my parents aged and their lack of muscle tone began to define the parameters of their lives. I don't want that for me and I don't want that for you. (*steps off soapbox, whispers, "please exercise"*)

• Now shade in one hour every day for breakfast and bathing. You may not actually do it at the time you shade in, but we want to account for that time. The specifics are not important just yet. Like with your outlining and writing process, you'll tweak your process and make it your own. Like if you're on a tight deadline, you may choose not to bathe. Perfectly fine … once in awhile.

• If you work at home, shade in an hour every day for lunch (that's actually 30 minutes for lunch plus two 15-min breaks). Realistically, it takes me about eight seconds to shove food in my piehole, but sometimes I do a crossword puzzle, or I actually cook something to eat, or I empty the dishwasher, or I get the mail, or I finish reading the newspaper. We're building in some 'just-in-case' time.

• If you work outside the home, shade in an hour for lunch on the weekend. If you work outside the home, you must promise to take at least a 30-minute lunch and two breaks every day *and leave your desk*. A million studies have shown you'll be more productive if you do so.

• Shade in one hour for dinner. That will include cooking-plus-eating OR eating-plus-cleaning. Unless you live alone there is no reason for you to both cook and clean. We'll revisit this concept when we discuss Delegation. Oh, yes we will.

• If you do the menu-planning and grocery shopping, pick a day and shade in one hour to plan your meals for the week, look up recipes, and make a grocery list. Then shade in another hour to do the shopping. Of course this can be on two different days. If you know it takes longer to do your shopping, then add the extra time. If you do food prep for the week, add time for that on Sunday, or whenever you typically do it. If you have someone who does these things for you, thank your lucky stars and just sit there looking smug.

• Because you're a writer, shade in an hour every day of guaranteed writing time, whether you're a full-time writer or not. If you get more as we shade in more spaces, great. But this way you know you'll get at least one hour, even if things get crazy.

• Now, hearken back to that list you made of stuff you

want to do regardless of time or money. Shade in one hour every day to tackle some of the things on that list. That's filling your cup with "Me Time." Me Time never includes any of the things we've already accounted for. Use your Me Time to do what you love. Your Me Time and your exercise time are the things you're going to be tempted to blow off. But don't. They're non-negotiable and you need to treat them as if they were your most important meetings every day. Trust me. You think it's counter-intuitive to be adding these things in if you weren't doing them before, but they really will help to create the balance that I know you're craving … otherwise you wouldn't be seeking advice.

Again, the exact times you shade in are less important than just in blocking out the hour. If your list included *read more for pleasure*, *take a Danube cruise*, and *learn to tap dance*, then realistically, you may not be able to do that every day in the 6:00 a.m. block of time you shaded in. But when you're setting your actual schedule, maybe on Monday, Wednesday, and Friday you decide to read from 6-7:00 a.m.; on Tuesday you research tour companies and study maps of Eastern Europe from 8-9:00 p.m.; and on Thursday from 5-6:00 p.m. you take a tap class. (If you work up a sweat, you get to count this as exercise time too … squee!)

• Shade in an hour on Sunday to debrief the past week and plan the next one. As you get better at this, it won't take an hour, but we'll allow for it in this exercise.

• Now put in anything else you know you have to do at a certain time like if you volunteer every Tuesday at the food bank or if you go to church on Sunday. Keep in mind that some of these things might also fill your cup and count for some of your Me Time.

• Shade in one hour a day for predictable, regular things like helping with homework, laundry, housework, yard work, bill paying and such. Again, you may not do yard work for an hour each day, you may choose to do a 3-hour block of time on Saturday, but I want you to be able to account for that time. And, of course, while you're helping with homework, you might also be paying your bills and running the washer and dryer.

• Shade in at least 7 hours for sleep and/or self-care. If you have trouble sleeping, please try and do something that falls under the category of "self-care." It's probably tempting to think since you're not sleeping you may as well tackle some of those household chores. But I bet watching a movie, or reading, or taking a long, relaxing bath might be better for you. It would certainly be more fun!

Now take a look at your white space. Do you have a lot? Just a little? None?

If you don't have much, try to figure out why. But more importantly, try to figure out how to get more of it.

Can you eat lunch in a conference room at work or in your car while you write or get in some Me Time?

Can you rejigger some of these illustrative shaded-in hours on paper into something more in tune with your reality, like getting a right proper workout (20-minute high intensity intervals!), bathing (2-minute boot camp showers!), and eating some breakfast (power bar!) within a single hour rather than the two we accounted for here?

Can you free up some time for yourself by taking public transportation to work so you can write instead of drive?

Can you drive to work an hour early and park yourself at a nearby diner and write? You might even get more than an hour if it means you'll miss your typical rush hour drive. Same with coming home. Those two hours might actually turn into three hours of writing time. If you want to try this, I would suggest that you don't go into the office early. I guarantee you'll get interrupted. But the only interruption you'll get at a diner is a welcome coffee refill. Maybe pancakes.

If you work long hours, can you give yourself permission to leave after your 8-hour shift?

Can you hand over to someone else the menu-making, the

grocery shopping, and/or the meal prep? Or pay for one of the food delivery services?

If you don't have a lot of white space in your schedule, then you need to stop right here and rethink some things because we haven't even addressed your To Do list yet. I know you're tempted to delete that exercise time or lop off a couple of hours from your sleeping time. I understand the temptation, really I do, but I also want you to create a satisfactory system for you to get everything done that needs to be done without exhausting yourself.

There are many, many stories of successful authors who cut waaaay back on their sleep to get their books written. That may be fine temporarily, but it's simply not sustainable without risking your health and maybe your relationships or day job. So I would really prefer if you found some other, more creative ways to free up your time.

Take some time here and see what you can do. Download another copy of the weekly planner and try again. When you're comfortable with the amount of white space on your schedule, then move forward again.

This is the basic framework for your week.

33

LET'S TALK ABOUT THOSE
NECESSARY BUT PESKY TO DO LISTS

Raise your hand if your To Do list is a mile long every day and you can't get it all done. This happens to me more often than I should admit. Often it's because we're doing things we've never done before and we don't know how long they'll take so we over-schedule. It's an easy fix, though, but it requires homework.

To figure out how long something takes, time yourself doing the task three times as you normally would. This may take a while to compile. For instance, I started using new software to manage my mailing list and newsletters. But I only send newsletters once a month, if I'm really bringing my A-game. So it will take me at least three months to figure out how long I should allow to produce each one. But it's something I will continue doing, so I should try to determine how much time it takes. Of course, the more I'm in the software, the faster I learn it, but also, the more nifty things I see I can add in. Sigh. A conundrum.

When you're timing yourself, be sure to include any time sucked up by interruptions because interruptions are inevitable.

When you've timed yourself three times, add them together and divide by three. This is the average amount of time this particular chore takes you to complete. With this information you don't have to guess anymore and can schedule accordingly.

Of course, some things we only do once, so we just have to use our best guess and strictly hold ourselves to the time we allotted ourselves for the task. If it takes two hours but you only allowed for one, then you'll have to complete the task tomorrow. Keep in mind that you can and should revisit the times for things you do often. When I had all three of my kids at home, grocery shopping took at least two hours. Now with just me and my husband, it's about thirty minutes. Likewise, the more I do those newsletters, the faster I get them done.

Our To Do lists can overwhelm and stress us, often sucking the joy from the very fiber of our beings. But don't let them.

Decide tonight what your most pressing task is tomorrow and do it first. If tomorrow flies out of control, what one thing will make you breathe a sigh of relief that it's done? Get that to the top of your to-do list. Chisel it in stone. Even with all that chiseling, your stress is miraculously reduced.

You need a plan for your day or your week that determines when to do what. I don't have to tell you that a 'to-do' without a 'when' doesn't get done. But it's not how many hours you put in ... it's how much you accomplish.

Your To Do list can be as simple as listing one big thing, three medium things, and five small things to get done each day. BAM. Your list is done. Easy peasy.

Or it can be more complicated. It's completely up to you. It depends on how your brain works and how your life is. I like specifics in my life. I like knowing what I should be doing at 10:00 a.m. every Tuesday. That might drive you nuts, though, if you like a more free-flowing day.

My days are pretty much the same, so that schedule we shaded in looks basically the same for me from week to week. Understand that your day-to-day schedule can look wildly different each day. And that's fine. That's your life.

I do a lot of different things. I write mysteries. I'm involved with many social media platforms and blogs. I make purses out of recycled books and board games. I publish books both traditionally and independently. I'm my own full-time marketing/PR person. My husband and I own a print shop. I'm involved in my Sisters in Crime chapter, and my Mystery Writers of America chapter. I do an annual fundraiser for foster kids. I'm the Household Manager, which means I do much of the shopping and all the bill paying. I organize all of our theatre outings and vacations. I attend to 98% of the needs of our adorable and quirky dog. I have three kids strewn around the world. And I walk all the way across the street to the mailbox on days it isn't too hot/too cold/too rainy/too snowy/too windy.

I'm no different from you, although our specifics are different.

I'm crazy busy but I love doing all of it. Of course it spins out of control very easily. I've learned I'm more productive if I set aside large blocks of time devoted to one thing. Friday afternoon is my "Making Purses Time" but a while back, I spent a very fun week only working on purses. No writing, no marketing, very little bathing. And when I was switching over my "So Seldom It's Shameful" newsletter to that new vendor, I focused on that for at least a solid week. Before I travel to mystery conventions or writer's conferences I need to spend an inordinate amount of time getting ready for that … creating swag, organizing meet-ups and ancillary sightseeing, dealing with travel issues, finding grown-up clothes that fit. So this schedule can be a flexible way to organize your life.

However, I know myself well enough to know I get twitchy if I deviate from my schedule too often. If I haven't written any blogs, or accomplished any marketing tasks, or worked on a book all week, I get a tad anxious. Getting out of your normal routine once in a while can be absolutely delightful …… until it gets too stressful.

Know that you will absolutely have emergencies regardless of how carefully you structure your plan. Your plan is designed to work most of the time. (Just like your outline allows for some creative wandering off the path.) But when your kid has to go to the ER, or your car breaks down, or you have a bathroom remodeled, do what you can to get back on track as soon as possible.

That To Do list can be a real bear, though. It can also make you feel guilty and very, very bad about yourself, especially if you transfer the stuff you didn't get done from one day to the next, over and over again.

There's a solution for that, and it's so simple you'll kick yourself for not thinking of it yourself. Be like Elsa from "Frozen" and let it go.

Learn to be okay with what you didn't accomplish today. Just that little paradigm shift in your thinking can change your relationship with those 24 hours you're gifted every day.

Let go of stuff you'll never get to. Holding on to those tasks means guilt, frustration, and disappointment. The three worst gifts of the Magi.

Lighten your load by:

• deleting (what's the worst that can happen if you don't do it?)

• delaying (not procrastinating, but rescheduling for a better time)

• delegating (is there someone who can do it better, faster, cheaper, or good enough?)

• diminishing (shortcuts or shaving down the chore)

Where should you keep this holiest of sacred documents, you might ask, and what form must your calendar/schedule/To Do list take?

However you keep track of your list is fine as long as it's ALWAYS in one place. No sticky notes, no back of paper napkins, no computer list upstairs plus a handwritten list downstairs. No multiple calendars for everyone in the household. **One calendar in one place.** Everyone adds to it and refers to it daily. If everyone needs to use their phone to screenshot the calendar hanging in the kitchen every morning, then so be it. And if it ain't on the calendar, it ain't gonna get done. Their failure to write it down does not constitute an emergency on your part. Learn 'em up good and learn 'em up early. (But know it's never too late to insert a new household rule.)

The stuff on your calendar needs to get on your To Do list. I can do that once a week, during the time I set aside on Sunday, but if you have a busier household you might need to do it every day.

Electronic vs paper? Doesn't matter, but if you have large sloppy handwriting don't use a daytimer with tiny boxes to write in. If you're a Luddite, don't think you will be successful with a calendar app on your flip phone.

Set aside 15 minutes at the end of every day to make or review your plan for the next day.

Then during your debriefing time on Sunday, contemplate whether your week was successful. Why or why not? What will you do differently next week? What worked great that you'll continue to do and build on?

Then think about the week to come. What are the three most important things you want to get done next week? How will you make that happen? What might get in your way? Do you have a Plan B in case something (or someone) gets in your way?

Here's what I do. My pre-printed template is made from the timeline like we shaded in. All the things I want to accomplish every week are on this page.

I like the template idea so I don't have to reinvent my wheel every week. But I do revise the template every so often, usually when I realize I don't have everything accounted for any longer, or when I decide to change up when I do something.

You might have cracked the Becky Code and figured out by now that I don't like to do things at the last minute. Nor do I like to have to remember them.

Below is what my schedule/To Do list/calendar (I refer to it all these ways) looked like on a recent Monday morning.

		8:15 Dentist			
MONDAY	**TUESDAY**	**WEDNESDAY** CLEANING DAY?	**THURSDAY**	**FRIDAY**	**SATURDAY**
5-6:00 coffee/Nala/fb 6-7:00 read 7-8:00 treadmill 8-9:00 shower/paper 9-11:00 write *Solitaire*	5-6:00 coffee/Nala/fb 6-7:00 read 7-8:00 yoga 8-9:00 shower/paper 9-11:00 write *Solitaire*	5-6:00 coffee/Nala/fb 6-7:00 read 7-8:00 yoga 8-9:00 shower/paper 9:00 pay bills/errands · Nala - groomer toenails · body shop estimate · organize backpack folder · Dad's speeches	5-6:00 coffee/Nala/fb 6-7:00 read 7-8:00 treadmill 8-9:00 shower/paper 9-11:00 write *Solitaire*	5-6:00 coffee/Nala/fb 6-7:00 read 7-8:00 yoga 8-9:00 shower/paper 9-11:00 write or workshop *purses*	5-6:00 coffee/Nala/fb 6-7:00 read 7-8:00 tap/treadmill/yoga 8-9:00 shower/paper 9:00 menu/grocery list 7:00 Comedy Club tix - dinner · Dad's speeches? · backpack folder?
11-12:00 lunch/crossword 12-2:00 write *Solitaire*	11-12:00 lunch/crossword 12-2:00 write *Solitaire*		11-12:00 lunch/crossword 12-2:00 write *Solitaire*	11-12:00 lunch/crossword 12-2:00 write or workshop *purses*	
2-2:30 email 2:30-4:30 marketing calendar · Schedule 4 "What Is it" photos · brainstorm blogs for Puzzling Ink	2-2:30 email 2:30-4:30 marketing calendar · NL	· basement curtains	2-2:30 email 2:30-4:30 crosswords for LCC swag	2:30-4:30 marketing calendar	**SUNDAY** Grocery store early Broncos 2:00 clean oven
6:30-7:00 exercise			6:30-7:00 exercise		

THE NOTES I'VE HANDWRITTEN IN ARE WHAT I'VE ADDED TO MY schedule during my time on Sunday afternoons—the *specific* writing I'm going to do (work on my Solitaire novel), the *specific* marketing tasks (giveaway, templates, editorial calendar), the *specific* chores and errands for Wednesday (dog to the groomer, household paperwork to organize, basement curtains to fix), the *specific* things from my calendar that week (dentist appointment, comedy club tickets).

I'll cross them off as I go. You'll see on Saturday I've re-listed a couple of things with a question mark after them. That's because I'm pretty sure I won't get them done on Wednesday because they're both fairly big jobs. By adding them on Saturday, too, I give myself another block of time to complete them and I make sure not to accidentally fill Saturday with some other time consuming chore.

What about the things I don't get crossed off during the week? What do I do about them? Well, I can tell you those basement curtains may never get washed and hemmed. I didn't add it to another day or transfer it to next week's calendar. (I know this because they're still dusty and unhemmed as I edit this manuscript.) Those curtains are just not important to me. Maybe in six months they'll rise in importance. On the other hand, if I didn't get Nala to the groomer to get her toenails clipped, I would have added that to next week's calendar because that is important. Not desperate, mind you, but it does need to get done. And the body shop estimate? It was for minor damage when some thousand-year-old man made direct eye contact with me, then hit my rear bumper anyway. I wasn't interested in making an insurance claim for it, but I wanted to know if there was anything we needed to do to mitigate the damage. I probably asked my husband to take care of that for me. It's my car, but more his wheelhouse.

So that's how I use the shaded-in planner to make my preprinted template schedule which turns into my To Do list every Sunday. I look at what didn't get done last week and what needs to get done next week. All in one place.

On my website you can download an editable template schedule for yourself. Play with it until you get a weekly schedule you can live with, accounting for everything we shaded in. Start using it and tweak it until it meets your needs perfectly.

If you have trouble crossing items off your To Do list, you might benefit from having one or more Accountability Partners. These are people you check in with regularly, whether it's every day or every week. You share your goals and you hold each other accountable for accomplishing them. Just like when you're in a critique group for your writing, if you don't show up with new pages to share or insightful comments on their pages, you've let down the group and yourself.

In an accountability group, you're going to feel awful if you have to say you didn't meet your word count goal or whatever because you fell down the rabbit hole of watching cupcake decorating tutorials on YouTube. I'm guessing you'll only do that once because to admit it out loud is heart-breaking.

On the other hand, when you boast to your accountability partner(s) that you exceeded your word count goal, your buttons will pop with pride.

These accountability "meetings" are just quick check-ins by phone or Skype. Your group can choose to check in however makes sense, but I'd counsel you to not use email or text. You need to hear yourself say you did (or didn't) meet your goals. Plus, with email or text, you're going to be tempted to massage your message, perhaps shading the truth about your week, or offering excuses. But in real life, you won't want to hear yourself fibbing to a friend.

You don't have to "fix" anyone if they didn't meet their goals, nor do they "fix" you. You just need to hear how everyone did or didn't meet their goals, then listen to their new plan going forward. It's very effective for a lot of people.

It can, of course, turn into a coffee klatch, which is not productive, unless that's part of the way you've organized your group. Maybe you agree to talk longer on Friday night to catch up with each other's family stuff, or to hear about their fantastic trip, or to tell them about some thriller that kept you on the edge of your seat. But the daily check-ins are held to five minutes with no small talk … just the business at hand.

If you're looking for Accountability Partners, join the "Eight Weeks to a Complete Novel" Facebook group and ask if anyone wants to join you. (We can also use the group to brainstorm any time management or writing issues you might be having.)

And don't forget the power of a well-placed sticker on your calendar when you meet your goals. It worked when you were in kindergarten and it will work today. Did you write as many words as you promised yourself today? Then you get a sticker! Did you cross everything off your To Do list? Sticker! Did you focus on a big, important task for an hour? Sticker! Did you set your timer when you went on Facebook? Sticker!

It might sound silly, but you'll be surprised how proud you feel when you see your monthly calendar filled with stickers or gold stars that show you are accomplishing what you want, breaking bad habits, starting new habits, and moving closer to your goals. It's a cheap and effective visual representation of your ever-increasing wins.

If you have a challenging family who, in the past, made it hard for you to accomplish your goals, involve them in helping you attach those stickers. You'll be a good role model for them as they reach for *their* goals. Plus, they'll see the joy they are giving you by getting on board to help you reach your goals, or at least by not actively thwarting or sabotaging you.

So, back to the calendar you were shading in. Let's finish up with that white space. That's where your To Do list items go: all those things that need to be done once in awhile like dentist appointments, or shopping for a new stove … or if you work for yourself, all of your work activities that you haven't shaded in yet.

But what if, even after tweaking it earlier, you still don't have any white space? Don't despair. I have some tricks and tips coming up that might help you free up some of that space. But you're going to have to help. You're going to have to keep an open mind, and be honest with yourself about the different ways you might be sabotaging yourself.

Take a look at the "Weekly Planner With Times" you shaded in. Study it for a minute. Do you have a good balance of everything I asked you to shade in? If not, do it again. If you didn't do it in color before, go dig up some crayons or colored pencils and give it a whirl this time. It's so much more obvious in color.

Now that you know the end result of this coloring in exercise, tweak it as necessary until you make time every week for work, writing, sleep, things that fill your cup, and all the little things that add up to a fulfilling life.

When you're happy that you have a livable, workable timeline for your week, then download a copy of the "Weekly To Do List/Schedule." It's just a Word doc, so you can type directly into the document your specific, perhaps aspirational, week.

Since you're new to this, I suggest you type the actual times you shaded in for each block of time. Start at the top with when you wake up every day. Look again at my example. Leave spaces under the items where you might have specific tasks. For instance, leave space under your writing time to jot down the specific project you're working on. Leave space under any blocks of time for marketing, errands, "Me Time," exercise, and the like, so you know what you want to focus on during those times.

When you're happy that your "Weekly To Do List/Schedule" is something doable you can live with—or at least use it as the first step in your experiment—save it to your computer and print out a few copies. Use this template every Sunday afternoon, or whenever you will plan your upcoming week. Sit down with it now, no matter what day of the week it is, and pencil in the specific tasks you need to accomplish before your regular planning day rolls around.

Jot down the weekly items from your calendar on to this page. Little Billy's piano recital. Dentist appointment. Oil change for your car. PTA meeting. Conference call. Spouse's birthday.

Use it for a couple of weeks to get a feel for your new system, then tweak as necessary.

Pretty soon you'll have a weekly schedule that makes sense for you that you won't have to think about too much, but that will serve as a reference to keep you on track.

Any time life throws you a curveball, or when you get better at organizing or setting priorities, you can revisit the shading-in exercise and update your To Do List/Schedule.

It's an organic document that can change as often as you do. During the first few weeks using a schedule like this, though, pay very close attention to the times and activities you put on there. A document like this—just like a road map or sheet music or architectural plans—won't do you any good at all if you never refer to it.

34

SPECIFIC TIME MANAGEMENT PITFALLS AND SOLUTIONS

I WANT YOU TO START THINKING OF YOUR DAY AS **MORSE CODE dots and dashes**—dots for quick tasks, dashes for longer things that require concentration. Email is a dot. Writing your manuscript is a dash. Lunch is a dot. Planning your weekly menu is a dash.

Spend that first important hour of your work day concentrating on your most important task. But what if you can't concentrate that long? Your goal is for one hour of dash time, but if you can only concentrate for ten minutes, that's okay, but for every new 'dash period' add five minutes until you get to an hour. Anything more than an hour is counter-productive, though. You'll need at least a 5-minute break by then.

Some of us have the opposite problem. Do you ever get into The Zone with your writing or some other project and finally look up to see it's September all of a sudden and you've grown a beard? Me too.

That's perfectly fine if you didn't have anything else to do, but how often is that the case? A simple kitchen timer is your best friend. I use mine constantly. I set it for an hour during my dash periods so I remember to stop, stretch and check my to-do list. I set it when I check my email or Facebook (unless

I'm doing those in front of the TV). I set it when I call my daughter or else we talk for four hours. I set it to remember to eat my nine meals a day. Why, yes, yes it does sound like the NASDAQ trading floor at my house. But if I didn't use my timer, I'd be looking at the clock every eight seconds, worrying that I'll get in The Zone when I can't afford to, or that I'll starve to death and they'll find my sad skeletal remains in a little heap under my desk.

We talked about this earlier, but I want to reiterate that if you're addicted to your phone, you absolutely CANNOT use the timer on your phone. You must get a kitchen timer and put your phone far away from you, and turned off. No beeps, buzzes, or notifications of any kind.

But what if you realistically can't get one-hour blocks of dash time and you have some huge tasks?

Then you need to break down your task into bites that can be done in shorter sprints. Focus on completion. Your task won't be *work on my novel*, but rather *research how this Civil War weapon fired … write backstory for that character …. sketch out the inciting incident … find/replace all adverbs in Chapter 7.*

I subscribe to an online yoga studio and there's a class I like to do where the instructor says about yogic-style push-ups, "If you can only do one today, you do one." That's how I feel about all my tasks during the day. If you can't conjure up the energy to write for an hour, you can probably do thirty minutes. If you can't bear the thought of doing all the dishes, you can soak the gross pans. If you can't clear all your email, at least you can delete the junk.

Forward progress is what we're after.

If you take a quick break during dash time, do NOT check your email or social media. Instead, hula hoop or dance to a favorite song. Physical movement improves concentration.

This is a good time to talk about **Email.** If I haven't already, this is where I turn into your bossy, judgy best friend who bombards you with tough love.

Email is a big problem for me and I don't really get that

much. I can't imagine what it's like to be bombarded by hundreds of emails every day. Email is one of those technological things that is as much of a curse as it is a blessing. I love that I can shoot somebody a quick message at any time of the day or night and not worry about interrupting them. I also don't want to spend a ton of time chitchatting and hearing about little Billy's spelling bee. Don't get me wrong, I want to hear about little Billy's spelling bee, but over on Facebook, or at happy hour, or during a long, leisurely lunch.

Never check your email first thing in the morning. If you do, you'll be tempted to reply to some of it. The same thing holds true for checking email right before you go to bed. Just like with training your family and friends to respect your writing time, you need to train the people who email you.

If you reply to email first thing, chances are very good the person will respond back to you immediately. And then you'll have to respond to that. Lather, rinse, repeat and your morning (and thus your schedule) is shot.

If you reply at midnight, you're training your emailers that you will answer emails at all hours. They will take advantage of that and feed their addiction to urgency. Just because they think it's urgent does not mean you must.

Whatever time you typically reply to emails is the time you're training people to expect your replies. That's why I advocate you set up your email block of time for early afternoon. That way you have a large dash of morning to focus on whatever you need to focus on, and possibly complete, that day. Very rarely does email rise to that level of commitment. Email should never sap that much of your energy and brain space.

The other reason not to check your email "real quick" before you get on with the important tasks of the day is that it ALWAYS takes longer than you expect. In no time at all, your "real quick" check just ate up 30 minutes. Unless you scheduled that 30 minutes, it's now been stolen from something important. You don't get it back.

Change the rhythm of your day by starting with long dashes. Leave short dots for later when your brain is tired. Your goal is to be in charge, but email by its very nature means someone else is in charge. Other people rarely—as in "never"—have your best interests in mind. Even important emails can wait a few hours.

Only check your email at times you designate. During that time, respond immediately to the ones that will take you less than two minutes. That's a dot. If it requires longer, that's dash time and needs to be scheduled at a specific time later that day or even on a different day. I don't like to deal with email on my phone because it's almost guaranteed I'll be sending the results of my urinalysis to my entire networking group. Many people have better trained fingers than I do, allowing them to respond to email on the go, perhaps while stuck in one of those post office lines or traffic jams we talked about earlier. Admittedly, email access on your phone is another of those technological combo blessings and curses.

If all else fails and you feel overwhelmed by your email, declare Email Bankruptcy and delete it all. If it was important, you'll hear about it again. In an NPR interview with Terry Gross, I heard Biz Stone (the founder of Twitter) say he does this. He apparently has a low threshold of information overload, which I find hilariously ironic. But if you've emailed Mr Stone and he never responded, that's probably why.

If the founder of Twitter doesn't feel it necessary to be connected 24 hours a day, neither should you. Productivity tools should serve us, not the other way around.

Your email provider should have some of those productivity tools to help you. Investigate them. Set up folders to organize your email before you even see it. Have a folder for "family" that you look at immediately. But if Uncle Leo sends you long emails of Dad Jokes, shuttle him into the "ain't nobody got time for this" folder. Set up folders labeled "boss" or "publishing professionals" or "critique partners" or whatever makes sense for you.

If you're carbon copied on a lot of emails, set up a "cc" folder.

As I type this, it makes me wonder … do young whippersnappers even know what a real carbon copy is? It's funny how we still keep the original names for things that have no actual bearing on the world today. Dialing a phone. Rolling down a car window. Taping a show.

I'm reminded of the time we took our kids on a road trip and found ourselves at one of those country museums that had a jumble of old farmhouse "antiques," most of which could be found at my house.

Anyway, back to your "cc" folder … if you're not the main recipient, then see what happens if you don't read them. I bet you're not going to miss a thing. If anyone complains, you are well within your rights to say you thought it was for information only. If the email is in your folder, all you have to do is a quick search to get up to speed on whatever the issue is.

If you make your email provider sort your emails for you, then you get to decide which to read, in what order, for your specific amount of time.

The "archive" function in Gmail is very useful. You can archive if you don't want the glorious feeling of deleting, and everything is still there if you need to search for it. But you *won't* need to search for it because if it *was* important, whoever sent it will email you again. But they *won't* email again because whatever they emailed you *before* wasn't that important and they immediately forgot about it. Just sayin.

If you're in any email groups, make sure your settings are on weekly or daily digest. Never get individual messages on those things if you can help it. When you get your digest, all your have to do is look at the topics and see if any of them are really of interest or necessary for you to read. I subscribe to a lot of groups, but it's rare that I actually read one of the digests in its entirety. If there's a topic that intrigues me, I can click on that particular message and go straight to it, bypassing the others that don't apply to me. In the follow-up digests, if the same topic is still trending, you can again click just on that message thread, or if you got all the information you needed, delete it all again.

When your email is empty, you might be surprised how fiercely you'll fight for it to stay that way. Have you ever had your carpet deep cleaned? You didn't want to step on it afterward, did you? When you deep clean your email, you won't want anything in there. But once your email is empty, it's SO EASY to keep it that way.

Shuttle messages you might want to read later into folders. Delete everything that's unimportant. If someone sends you a "thank you" message about something, you don't have to follow up with a "you're welcome." Email isn't lunch with the Queen. Different etiquette rules apply. Plus, when you respond with a "you're welcome" email, you've just given your friend an email that THEY then need to deal with. If there's an email thread for forty-leven messages replying to a party invitation, don't read them! Save the original one with the pertinent details, reply immediately with your RSVP, put the date on your calendar, then archive it. Or do what I do and take a screenshot or print it so I know the address and time of the party without having to go into email to find it.

Here are my Five F Words to deal with email. (You'll notice I didn't take the obvious route. But you know I wanted to.)

- Face it
- Forward it
- Flag it
- Fling it
- Float it

Face it if it's just going to take a second and/or it falls with your scheduled email time. **Forward** it if someone else should handle it or is better equipped to handle it. **Flag** it if you can ignore it but are too nervous to **fling** it into the trash. **Float** it if you can schedule it for a more convenient time.

I heard someone once talk about "conserving your keystrokes." The gist was that in your life you have a finite number of keystrokes. Don't waste them on emails, which will probably only be seen once and then disappear—poof—into email heaven. Instead, if you have to tell someone three, or five, or twenty paragraphs of something, you are much better off to put that in a blog post. If one person needed that information, then the chances are good that more people will too. And do you really want to write those three, or five, or twenty paragraphs again? Wouldn't it be better for everyone if you can say, "Oh, hey, I wrote about that. Here's the link." Or write it in a Word doc that lives on your computer that you can just copy and paste, or attach.

Any email reply longer than half a dozen sentences should be in a blog post, or on your company's FAQ page, or in your profile or "about" information.

Of course, emails to your family might not fall into this category, but keep an eye on the emails you receive in the next couple of weeks. How many of them force you to repeat yourself? And what will you do about that?

Most email isn't critical and if it is, they should be calling you anyway, which is the perfect segue to talk about …

Cellphones are not at all a problem for me. I rarely have mine on. My cellphone is for me to take pictures of funny signs or my adorable dog, or update Facebook, or in case I get a flat tire, or I need to order a pizza, or find myself in other emergencies. My kids and my mother know to text me and/or leave a voice mail, otherwise I just assume they wanted to chat. If I'm trying to work, then I don't have time to chat. When I take a 5-minute break between tasks or at lunch or when the dog needs to go out, I check my phone for any voice mails. If I get a missed call but no voice mail from someone not in my contacts, that number gets gleefully blocked.

My daughter and I can talk for hours on the phone, so we make appointments where we clear our schedules and catch up. She's usually on a long walk in Oregon where she lives, and I'm sitting in Colorado on the patio or in my comfy chair with a glass of wine. When it's scheduled like that I never feel guilty or rushed. Both of us get some well-earned Me Time.

Sometimes I'll get a call with something important or time sensitive, but not very often. My kids and spouse are all grown-ups who went through my rigorous training.

I understand not everyone is as lucky (or strident) as I am about phone calls. (I even kept my landline so I can give out that number when I'm forced to. Guess whose cell phone gets very few spam calls?) But you need to treat phone calls like emails. First, if you're checking your phone during the very limited time you have to yourself, you're allowing everyone else to be in charge of your time. You're making their needs more important than yours.

You may need to retrain your friends and family to understand that "Between these times on these days I'm writing and I won't be looking at my phone. And sometimes I have, yanno, other stuff to do, so either call me at different times, or be patient until I get back to you, or—and here's something fun—solve your own darn problems!"

Just like with your email, make sure your notification noises are off, and only check your phone messages at designated times, making sure your regular callers know when that is.

Most cellphones have a "Do Not Disturb" setting, where only certain phone numbers can get through to you during certain times that you designate. The answering service on your on-call nights. Your parents. Your kids. That plumber you've been waiting to hear from. Figure out how to set this up on your phone.

Is call waiting still a thing? If so, get rid of it or turn it off. It's rude and rarely useful. It's another example of ill-conceived multi-tasking. There's no rule that says you need to be at everyone's beck-and-call, especially at the expense of whomever you're already talking to. By taking a second call, you're now wasting their time. Don't be *that* person.

Unplug during mealtime and insist your family does the same. This counts toward filling your cup. *Be present* when you have the opportunity to be present with people you love.

People complain about kids being on their devices constantly but I've seen tons of normally polite adults who whip out their phone to take a call or read texts when I'm out with them. (Hm. Maybe it says more about me being boring than them being rude, but even so … telling me I'm boring is rude, too, she pouted.)

I think the tide may be turning with kids, however, because I saw a story on the news not too long ago about a high school that decided to lock up everyone's phones at the beginning of the school day. They unlock them at the final bell and the kids love it. They said things like, "Everyone talked at lunchtime. It was so much fun!" Kids haven't lived in a world sans screens and were gratified to have the opportunity. I find that encouraging.

All this to say that your phone and your email are tools for YOU, not for everyone else in the world. You get to be in charge of them. You have the power, unless you give it away to every Tom, Dick, or Harry who wants you to do their bidding. Don't let them. Take back your power. Make your email and phone work *for* you, not *against* you. And for heaven's sake, turn them off when you want to write!

Social media is getting to be the same type of problem for otherwise normal, intelligent people. Like me. And you?

I'm not on a lot of different platforms on a regular basis, but Facebook is sometimes a problem for me. I loves me my Facebook! I don't play any games and I don't scroll through my entire feed anymore, but still.

The problem for writers is that social media is often part of our work day, so, just like with email and phone calls, we need to learn to tame it.

Social media falls into a gray area category in my schedule. First, it fills that 'hanging with people I love' role that we all need. But because Facebook [or insert your favorite social media site here] wants to make money, they keep changing their algorithms on us, making the site less and less useful to us freeloaders.

On Facebook, for example, they're going more to a paid platform, trying to get every business on there to buy ads. So regular personal profiles and business pages that don't buy ads get pushed waaay to the back, as far as visibility goes. However, they're pushing "groups" now (which, of course, can change in a hot minute), which is good for us in a time management sense. The groups are typically things you're interested in, so YAY! When you join or create a Facebook group, you automatically get a notification every time someone posts in there, depending on how you set up your notifications. You can set the frequency of notifications separately for every group you belong to.

I belong to some marketing groups, some mystery groups, groups for people using certain kinds of programs/software, and a group of amateur tap dancers. I've created a private group—Becky's Book Buddies—where my mystery readers can have direct access to me, and I've created a group for people who read this book or attend my "Eight Weeks To A Complete Novel" workshops and want to talk about issues surrounding writing and time management.

But a group dedicated to one topic leaves out your Aunt Boopsie's posts about her new monkey butler, and photos from that friend from high school who has the cool job at the forensics lab, and the hilarious memes that guy from work always shares.

Many of us use social media for fun *and* for work so we need to harness it properly to see what we want to see.

Social media can be addicting. By its very nature, the lure to keep scrolling "just one more" is very real. You must constantly remind yourself that if anything important happens in your world or the world at large, you will always hear about it. The information will bombard you from many different directions at many different times. You won't miss a thing if you shut off the notifications on your news site or favorite social media channels while you concentrate on what you say is most important to you.

On that list you made earlier about the things you wanted to do if money and time weren't an issue, I'd be very surprised if you said, "Read all the posts and comments on my social media feeds." I'm guessing, of course, but I doubt your social media consumption is more important than that book you want to write. So why give social media all that power?

For work, you need to curate the things you see and use. Join and create groups on Facebook, use the scheduling tools on Twitter, and strategically follow your industry influencers whether they're on Instagram, Pinterest, Linked In, Reddit, or wherever.

And always set your timer.

If you use social media only for fun, set your timer or scroll while you're doing something mindless, like watching comfort reruns on TV, or that football game that's not quite going your way, or while you're waiting for the water to boil for your spaghetti.

But let me say it again … at the very least, set your timer and shut off your notification noises. You don't need to get beeped at every time someone posts, comments, tags, or retweets. It's so easy to fall down that rabbit hole on social media. It's engineered that way. You simply can't help it. The addictive aspect is well documented. Remember that. These sites are doing everything possible to keep you scrolling, but you don't have to. No matter how many times you peek at your feed, you will never be "caught up" on social media. You will always miss something. Accept that. Consciously choose to remember those halcyon days when you were bliss-fully unaware of what your friends ate for breakfast, or where they went on vacation, or what their political bent was.

There are ways to deal with the lure of social media, some quite simple. Remove the app(s) from your phone. Don't allow the sites to save your password(s). Making it just the teensiest bit more difficult to log on may be the reminder you need not to do it so often.

Another easy thing to do is to jot down how many times and for how long you log in to your social media sites. Try it. I bet you're surprised (and perhaps horrified) at how often you visit. You wanted to "find extra time" in your day? It's probably there.

There are also apps that block your social media. Do an internet search for "apps that block social media" then install as many as you need.

When you make it just a bit harder to get to your account(s), you will think twice about going on there just to check "one quick thing," or if you're bored, or if you're avoiding something.

And speaking of **Procrastination** …

Researchers have found that 20% of the general population and a jaw-dropping 95% of students are chronic procrastinators. I'll stick my neck out and declare that 100% of humans are occasional procrastinators.

If I have to do something I don't want to do, I'll often bribe myself. "There's a piece of chocolate waiting for you after you make that call." If I focus on *this* for an hour, then I can do *that* for 10 minutes. (Set your timer!)

Tell yourself you only have to focus on a task for five minutes. When you're finished with those five minutes, the next five are easier. It's the same way we get on the treadmill. But when we tell ourselves we're going to run ten miles today, or write that chapter, or clean that closet, or learn Italian … well, then that's just *non buono* and isn't going to happen.

You'll find your project isn't as difficult as all the excuses, mental anguish, and self-flagellation. The feelings surrounding procrastination are *always* worse than the task at hand.

If you are a procrastinator, next week don't do anything differently, but keep a log. An honest one. Did you avoid all tasks or just some? See if you can find a pattern. Do you hate making phone calls? Did you procrastinate because you were hungry? Was it always at the same time of day?

After your brutally honest week, what were your conclusions? But more importantly, how will you fix it? Procrastination is a skill you learned, not a helpful one, mind you, but a skill nonetheless. Therefore it's a skill you can unlearn as well. Replace it with something that won't cause you so much angst and psychic energy.

Much of the stress in our life comes from thinking we're not doing stuff as fast as we should or getting as much done as we should. And the word "should" is very subjective. What "should" I weigh? How clean "should" my house be? How much "should" I listen to my co-workers? How much "should" I outline my novel? (Wait … I know that one!)

Procrastination costs more than just time. It also costs money, health, and happiness. We exchange procrastinating for guilt, regret, low self-esteem, and worry. Not a fair trade, in my opinion.

So why do we procrastinate??

• *We get a buzz from 'working our magic' at the last minute.*

• *We have trouble prioritizing*—if everything is a priority, then nothing is.

• *We have to do boring stuff that we don't wanna.* But that's an easy fix. Find something fun about it, or play your favorite music while doing it, or remind yourself that once it's done, you can move on to more entertaining tasks.

• *The job at hand is too big and we don't know where to start.* So break it down. You don't need to organize your entire kitchen, Marie Kondo-style. Just tackle one shelf. You don't write a novel all in one fell swoop. You write a sentence, then a paragraph, then a page, then a chapter ... over and over. You're not going to lose ten pounds this week and fit into your high school prom outfit, but you can replace that soda with water. Baby steps. Eating your elephant one bite at a time. Which also won't get you into that outfit.

• *Sometimes we procrastinate because we don't have enough time.* This is the one that can trip me up. I like to spend large chunks of time on projects so if I only have thirty minutes, I won't start. After our first child was born I went back to work and my husband stayed home with her. My office was nearby so I was able to go home at lunchtime. I was always amazed that my husband could be halfway done vacuuming the living room, have a sink full of dirty dishes, lunch in the oven, playing with the baby, and in the middle of a magazine article ALL AT THE SAME TIME! It truly blew my mind. When I stayed home with her, I'd have days where I never even got out of my jammies because ohmygawd, what if she woke up before I finished?? I never even knew this was a problem for me until I saw him in action. I've learned that I don't actually have to finish something in its entirety before I move on to the next thing, and can use the short time that I have to nibble the edges of a task.

• *Sometimes we procrastinate because we don't know where to start on a project.* When I write, I stop midsentence when I quit for the day or for lunch. It just takes me a minute to re-read a few sentences and get right back into it. I understand that not everyone is as linear as I am. Sometimes it's perfectly fine to just start anywhere. Lots of writers start with a particular scene that excites them or with the ending because it's so epic, and then they go back and write the transitional scenes.

• *If we don't care about the project we will definitely procrastinate.* That's an easy fix, too. If you don't want to paint the bookcase, don't do it. Either live with the old paint or get someone else to do it. As Mary Poppins would say, brushing her hands together, "Pish posh."

• *Fear of failure.* This is a biggie for lots of people, but when you think about it, it's pretty irrational. There really is no "failure." There's either succeeding or learning. So what if you don't succeed at something today? That seems like excellent knowledge to have. If you don't succeed, then you know right away you can't train a monkey butler/ tap dance on Broadway/ write a first person erotic cookbook set in Victorian outer space and you can move on to something else. So I'll give you the same advice my dad always gave me. *What's the worst that can happen?* If you fail, one of two things happens … you never have to do it again, or you learn something that helps you succeed so you can try again with the new and improved you.

• *We procrastinate by putting off jobs that are too difficult.* If that's something you're guilty of, then simply reframe your thinking about the task. Yes, it's difficult to write a novel, but not TOO difficult because people do it every day, even stupid people and if you're reading this, you're smart!

• *We'd rather be doing something else.* Well, duh. But we're grown ups. We do things we don't want to all the time. Nobody *wants* to change a poopy diaper or clean up dog barf or renew a driver's license, but we do it because it must be done. Of course, if you can delegate these types of tasks, that's even better, especially with regards to poopy diapers or dog barf. And we'll talk about delegation in a little bit.

Here are some of my favorite quotes about procrastination:

• *A year from now, you will wish you had started today.* *~Karen Lamb*

• *When there's a hill to climb, don't think that waiting will make it smaller.* ~H. Jackson Brown Jr

• *Twenty years from now you will be more disappointed by things you didn't do than by the things you did do.* ~often attributed to Mark Twain, but also one from H. Jackson Brown Jr

• *Procrastination is like a credit card: it's a lot of fun until you get the bill.* ~Christopher Parker

Clutter. Now I don't want to go all Marie Kondo on you, but do you still have videotapes but no VCR? Cans of soup with a 'use by' date before your kids were born? A closet full of clothes that don't fit? A drawer full of terrible manuscripts that should never see the light of day? A computer desktop so covered with folders, screenshots, and documents that you can't see your adorable desktop image?

Wave goodbye to all of them.

You need to declutter everything. All the rooms of your house. All of your drawers (how many spoons or pairs of socks do you really need?) All of your closets. Keep only the clothes that fit and make you feel great when you wear them. Declutter your car. Your writing work space. Your computer desktop. Your file cabinet. Your shelves. Pass along books that you're never going to read again. Get rid of all those dustables you've accumulated over the years. Save the ones that make you smile every time you see them AND that fit with your vision of your space. If need be, get rid of that too-convenient table or shelf you dump stuff on.

Know where to keep things and what system works for you. At the risk of sounding like my grandmother, I'll tell you to "use it up, wear it out, make it do, or do without" and remind you to find "a place for everything and everything in its place."

It's a huge waste of time to search for what you need. Your car keys should always go in the same place if they're not in your ignition. Your glasses live on your face or next to the coffeepot. Your mail gets sorted over the trashcan, then your unpaid bills go in your organizer. Everything you need for your meeting goes on the floor next to your shoes or in the car.

Declutter your brain too. Have you ever gone to bed and your brain starts spinning? Get up and write it all down, no matter how big or small. You'll sleep like a baby once your subconscious isn't worried about forgetting something. As a bonus, you've just written your To Do list for tomorrow.

Don't hang on to stuff because you think it might be worth something someday. Visit eBay and realize it won't.

If you can't bear to get rid of stuff, go for a Trial Separation. Box up clothes you don't wear, kitchen utensils, and your treasured dustables and put them in the basement or garage. Tape the box shut and write the date on it. If you need something from that box, you have my permission to retrieve it. But if the tape is still sealed in six months, donate it to a thrift store without even opening it. You haven't missed it and you don't need it. You probably don't even remember what's in it.

You've all heard the environmental folks say you should *Reduce, Reuse and Recycle*, but I'd like to add another one ... *Refuse*. As in refuse to buy any more stuff. Ignore commercials, don't buy in bulk, and put your money toward something more interesting than clutter—like a writer's conference or something on that list you wrote earlier.

Don't forget to clear out your emotional clutter, too. Go back to those goals you wrote. What's important in your life? If something isn't helping you reach those goals, you need to jettison it.

If spending more time with your kids was on that list, then maybe let go of the idea they must be in bed every night at 8:00 on the dot. Instead, read an extra book with them, pull out the Legos or the train set and give them another thirty minutes of you.

If the guilt of not writing your novel is giving you too much psychic pain, then maybe let go of your Netflix account or your television or your subscription to the *New York Times*.

If you're feeling overwhelmed by the world and your goal is to prioritize your mental health, then maybe delete your social media accounts, or meet up with your real life friends more often, or exercise more.

Which is an excellent segue to talk about **prioritizing**.

Determine your top priority for the day—the one you'd sacrifice everything else to achieve—and focus on it. Ideally, this is the last thing you wrote down yesterday so you don't have to think about it today.

Tackle your hardest job first or the one you've been putting off the longest. Save your favorite tasks until the end of your list so you look forward to them. This helps with procrastination too.

If you can't decide which of your Completely Important Tasks to tackle first, prioritize like corporations do. Figure out which task is closest to the 'revenue line' ... ie, that which makes you money.

If your goal is to quit your day job and be a writer who can pay the bills, should you put the final edit on your manuscript or should you outline a new one? Duh. Final edit is closer to making money than sketching out an idea.

But what if they seem equal? Market one of my mysteries or a nonfiction book? Pitch the new series to an editor or investigate self-publishing it? Create a new workshop about a craft topic or a business topic?

Ask yourself some questions to see if you can come to a decision:

- How long will each take?
- What's the return on my time investment?
- When's the deadline?
- Which will fill my cup with joy?

If they still seem fairly equal, then it doesn't matter which you do. Either is a perfectly fine choice and you can quit agonizing over it.

I stress out about this more often than I should. To relax a bit I tell myself that the world will keep spinning even if I prioritize the wrong task. The sun will still rise whether I decided to market a mystery or a nonfiction title. Again, reframe your thinking.

Let's talk about **perfectionism**. You may be very perceptive and have already realized this is one category I do not have a problem with. This is underscored by my ending the previous sentence with a preposition, something up with which some of you shan't put.

The crux of the problem is that perfectionists lack perspective about their projects. It's either perfect or it's crap, there's no in-between. If this is true for you, you must learn "selective perspective."

But learning selective perspective is as easy as answering a couple of questions.

Which of your projects and To Do list items really need to be perfect? Perhaps your query, or your manuscript, or getting your bills paid on time, or being on time to that doctor's appointment.

Which tasks can be good enough? Perhaps your house-cleaning, or brushing the dog twice a week instead of every day, or doing a high intensity 20-minute workout on your own versus an hour-long class, or choosing those store-bought cupcakes for the bake sale.

In the resources, I've listed a great novel by Allison Pearson called "I Don't Know How She Does It." The first scene is a mom 'distressing' a store-bought cake so the other moms won't snipe at her for not baking it herself. Very funny and illuminating.

If you have perfectionist tendencies, figure out who belongs to that inner voice you hear telling you stuff isn't good enough. Your boss? Your fifth grade teacher? Your mother? Then decide if they deserve space in your head. If they don't, call the bouncer and toss them out into the alley. If they're right that you could do better/ be more diligent/ remember how to parse sentences/ be nicer to your sister or whatever it is they're harping about, thank them for pointing out your errors, clap them on the back, and politely show them the exit. You'll be happy to plug their concerns into your Selective Perspective Machine.

Back away from a project if you've worked on it too long. There is a law of diminishing returns. How often have you revised a manuscript multiple times and then found yourself back to the original version? It's time to stick a fork in it … it's done.

Remember, by the time you've outlined, written your synopsis, edited, and polished, you've seen your manuscript many times. Trust your early readers to tell you if you're on the right track or not, and *then* work on revisions, after you get some impartial and detached feedback.

Regardless, you must impose deadlines on yourself. Something done imperfectly on time is always better than something perfect if it's late. Professionals don't blow deadlines.

Allow yourself the opportunity to do something poorly. Just do it. Are you afraid to start that short story because it might suck? Guess what! It's gonna suck. Do it anyway. You can't make it better until there are words on the page.

Recognize degrees of excellence. On a scale of 1-10, a 7 doesn't look much different from a 10 to most people.

Multi-Tasking. Earlier when I talked about my husband doing all those household things at the same time? I want to be very clear. He wasn't multi-tasking. He was tackling projects in the time he had available. He knew I'd be home for lunch at a certain time, so it had to get in the oven. He could soak the dishes while he cooked. He could vacuum a little bit until the baby woke up and wanted to play. He wasn't trying to do all those things simultaneously; he was just making use of his dots and dashes.

It's been pointed out to me that in normal households there'd be no vacuuming while the baby was asleep. But we're not normal. We purposely vacuumed at naptime because we didn't want to live in a house where a little noise bothered anyone. It worked, too. All my kids can sleep anytime, anywhere, no matter the chaos swirling around them.

Don't confuse multi-tasking with doing a lot of stuff. Multi-tasking is trying to do all those things at the same time.

It has been scientifically demonstrated that it takes four

times longer to recognize and process what you're working on each time you switch among tasks. Research has also found that multi-taskers have short-term memory loss; gaps in attentiveness; and a general inability to concentrate.

Your brain simply can't focus on two separate things unless one of them is completely mindless.

• People can watch a movie on Netflix while they're on the treadmill, but not while they're working a crossword puzzle

• People can read while they listen to classical music, but not while they listen to podcasts

• People can drive while the radio is on, but not when they're texting or talking on the phone

You can disagree with me about a lot of things, but if you don't believe me, then I suggest you scroll through your Facebook news feed while listening to the actual news. I'll bet you a gazillion dollars you'll have no idea what Lester Holt just told you OR what your BFF had for breakfast.

But even if you don't believe the research, think about it logically for a minute. If you have an hour to write but you take "just a quick minute" to check email or social media, you've lost that time. Poof. Gone forever. And it's not "just a quick minute." It's easily ten minutes and probably much more. Do that only once an hour during your workday, (yeah, right) and you've lost an hour or two from your allotted twenty-four hours, ten minutes at a time.

You can call it multi-tasking, but you're really just frittering away your focus.

People multi-task because they're worried. It seems better to work on everything so all of their tasks are half done. But you'd feel much more in control if half of your tasks were 100% done and you knew you had a plan to finish the other half.

Don't confuse activity with accomplishment. You and Sisyphus can push that rock upthe hill all day long, but if it never gets to the top, you haven't accomplished anything.

You don't accomplish anything when you multi-task, either. Focus on one job till it's done or your time is up. Then focus on another one.

Like, for instance, your **Paperwork**.

There are three ways to see if you have a problem with paperwork:

- Can you find things?
- Can other people find things?
- Are you out of space?

Every day use some of your short 'dot time' to put things away, deal with your mail, add that contact to your database, file that receipt.

Before we had computer desktops, we had actual desktops. A hundred years ago I worked in the claims department at a large insurance company. My desk always looked like Mount Everest. My co-worker's desk looked like a surgical suite. She worked on one file at a time, while I heaped everything I needed to get done every day into my woefully inadequate inbox. But of course I didn't get it all done, so tomorrow's stuff got piled up too. It seemed like I never got anything accomplished and it was frustrating. So frustrating, in fact, that I would bring files home with me to work on in the evening in an impossible fantasy where I'd magically get "caught up." Insurance claims didn't work like that, I finally realized.

But whether it's actual desk clutter or computer desktop clutter, it makes it hard to work. And it hurts psychologically too. On my actual desktop, I've learned to keep open only what I'm working on. On my computer desktop, when I get too many documents cluttering up my screen, it makes it harder to work, too, so I take five minutes and file subfolders into their parent folders. And if I have too many parent folders, I make a folder that says *Ay Caramba!* and shove them all in there. Everything is still available, but it doesn't hurt my feelings so much.

Don't let your paper filing pile up. It makes it that much

harder to find stuff. When you file this month's electric bill, pull out last month's and shred it. I used to wait until I couldn't cram anything else in the filing cabinet. Then it would take me hours I couldn't afford to clean it out. And my shredder didn't like it very much either. But now, I don't even notice the three seconds it takes to weed out the old stuff.

And if you don't have a file cabinet, as soon as you finish this book, go buy one.

Is there too much paper on your desk? Put it all in one pile then sort it into three categories: *Tomorrow, Next Week, Next Month* ... or *Now, Later, Never* ... or *To Pay, To Take Action On, To Cogitate Over* ... *Yours, Mine, Ours* ... *Bell pepper, Poblano, Habañero*. Whatever makes sense for you.

Put the most important pile on your To Do list and deal swiftly and completely with it. Then tackle the next most important pile. When your piles are all dealt with, never get into trouble like that again. Deal with your paperwork every day.

I heard once that the Queen of England receives a pile of important papers to deal with each day. In interviews she has said that if she doesn't handle it completely every day, she'd never get caught up. She does it on holidays and when she's sick, never missing a day. It's the bare minimum she sets for herself.

If putting on a bejeweled crown makes paperwork more fun for you, so be it.

Do you keep every single copy of your manuscript drafts? Get rid of all those previous drafts but make it fun. I enlist my husband to load up the fire pit so we can make s'mores using the heat from my many, many obsolete words.

And speaking of **Delegation** ... it comes in two delicious flavors; Insourcing and Outsourcing.

Insourcing is when you delegate to your spouse, kids, roommate ... people you live with.

Outsourcing is when you delegate to someone else like a housecleaner, gardener, researcher, freelance editor.

Insourcing is usually free, but outsourcing always costs something. It doesn't have to be money, though. Consider bartering. I hate housecleaning but I love to write, so I once made a deal to trade writing some marketing materials in exchange for monthly housecleaning. It was a happy win-win.

Make a list of stuff you hate to do. Can anyone do any of those things better?

What is your time worth? If you want to make money at writing, doesn't it make sense to get someone to watch your kids so you can have dash time to write?

Lots of people love ordering their groceries online and then just picking them up. Maybe you will too.

We have a mobile veterinarian who comes to our house to take care of our pooch. There's also a mobile groomer we could use. In this gig economy, lots of business tasks can be hired out to freelancers on sites like Fiverr.

Switch menu planning/food prep/clean up/laundry/yard work with your spouse or roommate a week at a time. Use that week to pound out tons of extra words on your novel.

Enlist your kids. You get the help you need, they get money, or a new challenge, or a new skill, and a sense of accomplishment. Remember that your job as a parent is to turn small people with absolutely no skills into large people who can take care of themselves and others. Do not shirk the duty of allowing them to clean your house and make your dinner.

Be sure to let go of any perfectionist tendencies you might still be harboring, though. Embrace the concept of Selective Perspective. Which of these delegated tasks have to be perfect and which can be simply acceptable?

Dinner must be edible, but the recipe can allow for their creative flair, or lack thereof. Dishes must actually get clean, but your precise way of loading the dishwasher matters not one whit. Floors must be vacuumed, but your route across the carpet isn't the only path to enlightenment.

That said, remember to monitor and mentor. It's a short step to nagging and micromanaging. Set expectations and parameters of the job ahead of time, negotiate if you must, then let it go. No one will do things the exact way you do them and that's okay, as long as the end result is acceptable. The sooner you start your kids (or spouse or roommate), the easier this will be. Remember to celebrate their success so it breeds more successes.

Do NOT fall for the old trick of them doing a crappy job and pretending it's the best they can do, hoping you'll get so exasperated you'll just do it yourself. Make them do it over until they hit the mark of the expectations they previously agreed to. They'll figure out you mean business, but not if you're wishy-washy about it.

Resist the urge to do the ten-minute job that's taking them four hours to complete. It's always much easier to tie your kids' shoes than it is to teach them to pull those loops tight. But, seriously, do you want to be tying their shoes when they're in college? Cooking their meals? Doing their laundry? Filing their taxes?

Do you have a problem saying No? Have you ever faked your own death so you could quit your volunteer position?

You have to decide if a project makes your heart SING or SINK. But even if it makes you sing, you have to say no if it will shatter your fully-loaded plate.

You can say no graciously, however.

First, acknowledge their request by not laughing in their face. No matter how ridiculous their request is, they're serious or they wouldn't have asked. Honor the process.

Second, address your own limitations. *I'd love to be in charge of the school book fair/ the writer's conference/ the company picnic/ Vacation Bible School, but I've already committed to something else.* (They don't need to know your other commitment is extra sleep and no stress-related diarrhea.)

Three, offer an alternative. Give them the name of some other sucker who hasn't learned to say no. Or because *clearly* you are much nicer than I am, give them a different time when you would be willing to put it on your schedule. But only if it makes your heart sing AND you have time for it.

Here are some actual words you can use to say no:

- *Thank you so much for asking, but I'm unavailable then.*
- *I'd love to work with you, but I just can't right now.*
- *It sounds like a terrific opportunity that I'm going to miss.*
- *That sounds fun, but I'm afraid I have to say no.*
- *I am honored you asked. Unfortunately, I already have a commitment that day. Thank you for thinking of me.*

Saying NO to someone else means saying YES to yourself. It's no different than saying no to that third glass of wine or your hundredth game of video poker. We must do what is good for us.

You don't need to make excuses or apologize or feel guilty. The sun will come up tomorrow if you don't work on the book fair or chair that committee.

Letting it go to voice mail is another way to say no.

Speaking of answering the phone ... I read a statistic that fifteen percent of the population of the United States interrupts sex to answer the phone.

At the office, sure. But at home??

This seems like the perfect time to talk about **interruptions**.

The first defense here is education. If my door is closed, I'm working. I've booby-trapped it so if you open it, figure out how you're going to get to the hospital cuz I ain't taking you.

Even my perfect husband—who supports everything I do but doesn't understand it—had to be trained. Because he's not a writer, he didn't understand until I explained to him that whenever he popped into my office to tell me he was running to the hardware store, or to ask where in plain sight I've hidden the mustard, or even if I needed an ice tea refill ...

I lost, at a minimum, ten minutes. If he did all three of these things, that's thirty minutes that I'll never get back. Luckily, he was a quick study, as were my kids.

When they were little, if I was writing, the rule was they couldn't bother me unless there was burning, bleeding or barfing. And the barfing was negotiable. Because gross.

We touched on this a little bit earlier when we talked about Me Time. First, you deserve time for yourself. Really! The world will not spin off its axis if your kid/ spouse/ parent/ PTA/ critique group/ boss doesn't get what they want from you this very moment. Calmly but emphatically tell them you'll talk to them in an hour or tomorrow or never. But right now? Nope, this time belongs to you. Don't squander it or let mean, demanding, selfish people steal it from you.

Set aside time when people have unconditional access to you, but be consistent and firm. And give them a bit of a heads-up … *I'm going to shut my door and write in about ten minutes. Do you need anything in the next hour or so?*

Practice your catchphrases:

* *I'm in the middle of something right now. How's 2:00 instead?*
* *This week is impossible, but next Tuesday works.*

Ask how much time they need from you. If you can spare it, set your timer and give it to them. Or say, "I can give you five minutes now, or fifteen minutes later," then set an appointment with them. If they tell you they only need five minutes but it goes longer, tell them, "Sounds like you need more time to do this justice." Then set a time convenient for you.

If interruptions are a problem for you, keep a log over the next week. Jot down who interrupted, how they interrupted (phone call, tap on shoulder, sobbing uncontrollably at your door), how long they interrupted, and how important it was. Then, schedule an intervention for them.

Making yourself unavailable teaches kids, spouses, and

employees to make their own decisions and empowers them. I think everyone needs to go away for a weekend alone every so often (say, to an out-of-town writer's conference) to teach their loved ones how to fend for themselves. You're not doing them (or yourself) any favors by always being available or bailing them out.

Sometimes we interrupt ourselves, so be aware of that, too. Put your silenced phone in a different room. Turn off the notifications on all your devices from all your apps. When you're writing, never stop to look something up—spelling, word choice, research—it all goes in those placeholder brackets we talked about earlier. Revisit those sections during your editing time. Never give up your momentum or lose your large block of dash time for something that can go in your shorter dot time.

Interruptions, however, are inevitable, which is why we pad our schedule with a little extra time here and there. The trick is to manage these interruptions as effectively as you can.

Distractions are first cousins to interruptions, but instead of being caused by other people, we tend to create our own distractions.

We're distracted by a lot of things ... social media, that pile of laundry we think we should do, emails calling our name, all the stuff we do while we procrastinate.

The key is learning to focus and prioritize, something we've already discussed. What's the one thing you need to get done this hour/day/week/month/quarter/year? How long will you need to focus to get it done? Maybe only five minutes, but maybe an hour many times over.

Look again at the weekly schedule you colored in. Where will this time come from? Do you need more? The beauty of your calendars and schedules is that they can be revised at any time for any reason.

I hope by now you've figured out some ways to increase

the white space because now it's time to shade in time for your To Do list items.

Earlier, I tried to stress the importance of having one calendar in one place. That's because your calendar—all the dentist appointments, car maintenance reminders, PTA meetings, and such—need to go on your To Do list for the day or week. You need to be able to schedule your day around these outliers, and you certainly don't want to forget them.

I have a weekly To Do list because, as an empty nester, my life is less complicated than some, but also because I like to be able to look forward at a glance and see what's happening tomorrow or over the weekend. That came in handy when we got a big snow storm that meant I couldn't leave the house to do the errands I had planned. It was easy to be able to switch some stuff around for a couple of days until I dug myself out.

Of course, if you have a job outside the home that you can leave for medical appointments during the day, or to volunteer at your child's school, then this block of time is less important for you.

But if you are your own boss, you need to be able to manage these appointments seamlessly in your schedule.

Here's how I handle my all-in-one-place calendar and To Do list. It's easy *and* simple. That's the key to any system.

I have a calendar that hangs on a nail in my kitchen. On it, I write all appointments and things I don't want to forget.

When my kids were young, they knew if it wasn't on the calendar, it wouldn't get done. They'd solemnly hand over a birthday party invitation and watch to be sure I put it on the calendar. After recording it on the appropriate day, the actual invitation (or flyer, or email, or coupon, or newspaper blurb, or tickets, or whatever....) gets impaled by the nail the calendar hangs from. Everything is all in one place and I never have to search for directions, times, or details.

I've talked about this already, but every Sunday I make my weekly Schedule/To Do List from this calendar. That birthday party goes on it, but so does "Buy present for birthday child" a few days before.

I've recently changed my preprinted Weekly To Do List/Schedule, like I said I do periodically as my needs change. Now, I have a block of time I labeled "marketing calendar" three afternoons every week. I'm at a different place on my writing and publishing journey so I'm trying something new. It's all well and good for me to say I'll do "marketing activities," but much of the time I'm flummoxed about what, exactly, I should be doing. So I flounder, or worse, do something that doesn't really need to be done. (I am The Master at creating adorable and eye-catching memes I never use.)

Just having "marketing" on my schedule, however, does not magically fill me with perfect ideas. Nor does it fill the rest of the blocks of time.

So I've started using a separate calendar on which I write blog ideas and other marketing tasks. I schedule an hour, usually on the weekend or my early morning hours, and fill in at least two months of marketing tasks.

Because I know the launch dates of my books, I can also schedule obvious book release promotional tasks (blog tours, cover reveals, Facebook parties) months before the release, filling in the other days with more unusual or innovative marketing. Then, on Sunday, I will add these under my To Do List/Schedule under the white space set aside for marketing tasks.

I have a huge file of great marketing and promotion ideas, which, as you might have realized already, is both a blessing and a curse.

When my son graduated from Navy boot camp (where all his thinking was done for him), he had to outfit his own apartment. He called me from the aisle of trash cans at Target or someplace, completely baffled as to all the choices. "Mom, do I care how fast the automatic lid closes? Is stainless steel better than plastic? Has trash can technology lapped me … do

I need a motion sensor?" They all looked perfectly acceptable to him.

I feel the same discouragement when I thumb through my "Marketing" file. All the ideas are worthy and of interest to me, or else I wouldn't have kept them. But now, I'm determined to simply choose one for each day and whittle down that file.

This is what I hope you learn to do with all the information and ideas I've given you. Try something for a while, and then bend it to something that will serve you better as you change and grow as a writer and as a person, in your job and in your life.

If you work at home as a full-time writer, this is what you must do. There's nobody watching, ready to tap you on the shoulder if you turn on the TV in the middle of your workday "just for a sec." Only you can hold yourself accountable to do the difficult work of writing a novel, difficult work you say you want to do.

You must make time to do the difficult, the uncomfortable, the tedious, as well as the joyful, the empowering, the fulfilling. Roses have thorns, it's true, but it's equally true that thorns have roses.

35

IT'S ALL PERSPECTIVE

I'VE TRIED TO OFFER A BUNCH OF STRATEGIES TO HELP YOU wrangle your writing and tame your time management beast. But if you think you can't write faster, or follow an outline, or don't have enough time in your day, then you won't. Plain and simple.

How we spend our time is always a choice and we get to choose many times every day. We can choose to view time as a demon or an ally.

I know I told you earlier to think of your day as dots and dashes, but just for a little bit, I want you to think of your day as the trunk of a car. You CAN cram a lot in there, but you don't have to. You have the power to choose what goes in there. What do you want to haul around today? Do you just want to keep adding stuff every day without taking stuff out? Do you want to be done hauling it around early enough so you can play with your kids or do some writing? You're in control.

When you're feeling overwhelmed or swamped, just stop. Breathe. Stretch. Hula hoop. Laugh. See your friends.

My system of organizing, outlining, and writing is an amalgam of many things I've heard from many people over many years. Some things I tried immediately, some seemed way out of my comfort zone or capabilities, some things didn't make sense until I had more words under my belt.

We all need to find the way that works for us.

I've learned to think of my outline as my first draft. The skeleton I hang a body on … the dirt grid I plant a garden in … the blueprint from which my castle springs.

It doesn't matter your system of outlining, just that it works for you and you can quantify it. It took me some trial and error before I felt comfortable that my outline had everything I needed. I've developed it over several years and manuscripts in conjunction with my habits, personality, strengths, and weaknesses.

People laugh when I tell them I've developed a formula for writing. But I'm completely serious. I want a formula for writing … but not a formulaic story. Formulaic process, not product.

Like the way you get ready every morning. By now, you don't have to think about how you shower, brush your teeth, do your hair, get dressed, eat breakfast. You've developed a plan that works for you. But if you decide to go out for breakfast, or gel your hair for a change, or take a bath instead of a shower, you're still going to get out the door just fine.

It's the same way a good, workable, organic outline leaves room to follow tangents or rabbit trails. It still gets the job done.

I liken my outline to a vacation plan. I know we went to Poughkeepsie earlier, but now you're going from Los Angeles to New York City. You know the people who are going with you, and who you'll meet up with at the end. Maybe you know who you'll be meeting in Omaha, or maybe just *that* you'll meet someone in Omaha. Maybe you know you want to stop at the Grand Canyon, but you're not sure the route you'll take there. But maybe you end up at the Grand Canyon in the middle of the night, so that thing that has to happen ends up happening in Phoenix instead.

An outline can allow for organic spontaneous creativity—

and it should—but it must get your protagonist from CA to NY in the allotted time so all the things happen with all the people.

You can streamline your process, like I have, using whatever system makes sense to you, but know that as you get better, or more confident, or change genres, or something shifts in your personal life ... your writing changes too. Both in content and in method. So roll with those changes and always keep an open mind about other people's processes. See if you can steal a little nugget of wisdom that speaks to you. Make this system work for you. Use what makes sense right now and park the rest for some other time. Revisit it down the road. What doesn't work for you today might be exactly what you need next month or next year. Keep honing your process to make it the most efficient and useful for you.

You are smart, capable, talented, and realize the world needs your art. What's more important, though, is that YOU recognize you need your art.

Now go out there and make some.

RESOURCES

You can download the calendars I use from BeckyClarkBooks.com under the "stuff I teach" tab.

Join my "Eight Weeks to a Complete Novel" Facebook group to find accountability partners, ask questions, and have conversations about time management issues as well as writing issues.

Reminder of the 8 Weeks

Week 1 — outline and synopsis
    Week 2 — write
    Week 3 — write
    Week 4 — write
    Week 5 — write
    Week 6 — edit
    Week 7 — edit
    Week 8 — polish

Reminder of the ways of outlining we discussed

Blake Snyder's Beat Sheet
Eight movie reel scenes
Three Act Structure with plotting board
Write your three acts in prose form
Mind mapping
Character arcs
Libby Hawker's Three Legged Outline
Four Act Structure
Work backwards
The Story Circle
Mary Carroll Moore's "W" Plot Structure
Randy Ingermanson's Snowflake Method
Step outline
Leslie Karst's literal cut-and-paste
Chuck Wendig's Tent Pole Moments
Tell your story out loud
Checklist
Start with your synopsis
Expand your logline

Books

Rachel Aaron — 2K to 10K Writing Faster, Writing Better, And Writing More of What You Love
Jessica Brody — Save the Cat Writes a Novel
Joseph Campbell — The Hero with the Thousand Faces
J. Madison Davis — Novelist's Essential Guide to Creating Plot
Chris Fox —5,000 Words Per Hour
Malcolm Gladwell — Outliers (10,000 hour rule)
Libby Hawker — Take Off Your Pants: Outline Your Books For Faster, Better Writing

Randy Ingermanson — How To Write a Novel Using The Snowflake Method

Mary Carroll Moore — Your Book Starts Here: Create, Craft and Sell Your First Novel, Memoir or Nonfiction Book

Darcy Pattison — Novel Metamorphosis: Uncommon Ways to Revise

Allison Pearson — I Don't Know How She Does It

Victoria Lynn Schmidt — Story Structure Architect

Blake Snyder — Save the Cat

John Truby — The Anatomy of Story: 22 Steps to Becoming a Master Storyteller

KM Weiland — Outlining Your Novel

Chuck Wendig — Damn Fine Story: Mastering the Tools of a Powerful Narrative

Gotham Writer's Workshop's "Writing Fiction"

The Now Write series, edited by Sherry Ellis

Writing Mysteries, edited by Sue Grafton

Online

all of these URLs worked as of publication of this book, but you know how fast that can change. Links break, websites go away, articles get removed. I'll keep my fingers crossed they're still here when you're reading this.

- BeatSheetCalculator.com
- WorksheetWorks.com/miscellanea/calendars
- CalendarLabs.com
- RescueTime.com
- JamiGold.com/for writers
- *Shrunken Manuscript* —
https://www.darcypattison.com/writing/revision/shrunken-manuscript-2/
- *Biz Stone's NPR interview with Terry Gross* — https://www.npr.org/templates/transcript/transcript.php?storyId=133775340

- *Procrastination conference —*
https://www.nytimes.com/2017/07/21/science/procrastination-research-conference.html
- *The psychology of procrastination —*
https://www.verywellmind.com/the-psychology-of-procrastination-2795944
- *Chuck Wendig's thoughts about outlining —*
http://terribleminds.com/ramble/2010/06/01/story-structure-pitching-a-tent/
- *Tutorial about how to train Dragon Dictate —*
https://www.nakbaldron.com/7-steps-to-train-dragon-diction-from-mushu-to-smaug/
- *Mary Carroll Moore — "Your Book Starts Here: Storyboarding for Writers" —*
https://www.youtube.com/watch?v=pMhLvMJ_r0Y

ACKNOWLEDGMENTS

This book would only be half a book if it wasn't for the generosity of everyone who shared their outlining methods with me. Ellen Byron; Libbie Hawker; Randy Ingermanson; Leslie Karst; Ken Lee on behalf of Michael Wiese Productions and Blake Snyder; Mary Carroll Moore; Chuck Wendig; and all the other authors I've talked to over the years about their writing process. I've only given you a bare bones overview of their ideas, so please go read their books for the details.

There have been so many kind and generous writers who have taken my workshops and offered excellent feedback about the content over the years, but I'd like to give a formal thank you to my beta readers for this book: Rosemary Berry, Lindsay Maroney, Jessica Mehring, Kim Olgren, and Norma Thomas. I'm so very grateful for your insights.

Once again, my editor Jessica Cornwell has worked her magic on these pages, and I can't thank her enough for making me look like I paid attention in English class all those years ago. I'm pretty sure they've changed some rules on me over the years. That's my story, anyway.

And thank YOU for reading. I hope you've connected with something I've said and you can begin using it to move forward in your writing. It's ridiculously thrilling for me when someone tells me I've helped them in some small way.

Good luck with all your writing. May the literary gods smile down upon you!

ALSO BY BECKY CLARK

DUNNE DIEHL NOVELS (WITH TED HARDWICK)

Banana Bamboozle

Marshmallow Mayhem

MYSTERY WRITER'S MYSTERIES

Fiction Can Be Murder

Foul Play on Words

Metaphor for Murder (coming soon!)

CROSSWORD PUZZLE MYSTERIES

Puzzling Ink (Nov 2020)

Punning with Scissors (May 2021)

Untitled #3 (Nov 2021)

Subscribe to Becky's "So Seldom It's Shameful" newsletter for complete details on all her books, as well as giveaways, and other benefits only for subscribers.

Join the private group "Becky's Book Buddies" on Facebook for extra shenanigans.

BeckyClarkBooks.com

252551

TONI MORENO RIVERA

58006904R00102